Madogue Memories

Martin Neary

Copyright:

This is a book of my young memories and I have done my best to make them tell a truthful story. No names have been changed, no characters invented, no events fabricated. Although this book has been through the rigors of editing and meticulous proofreading, should any amendments be requested this will be done in the next printing.

Cover Design: *Jackie Kelly, "Scribes and Scribblers Ink"*
Cover Drone Picture: *Ciaran Murray, Charlestown*
Back Picture of Martin: *John McHugh, Kiltimagh*

Martin Neary

Copyright © 2024 Martin Neary

All rights reserved

For those wishing to reference this book:

Neary, Martin. (2024) *Madogue Memories*: Self-Published.

Available from: https://www.amazon.co.uk

DEDICATION

I dedicate this book to my parents,
Martin Neary from Drumshinnagh, Culmore
and Bessie Neary (nee Morley) from Madogue
and my two loyal four-legged friends
Van Gogh and Oscar Wilde

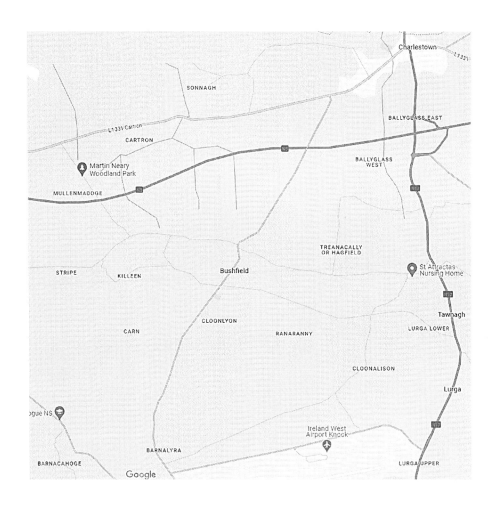

Source: https://www.google.com/maps

MARTIN NEARY WOODLAND PARK
Madogue
Swinford
Co Mayo
F12 N5D3

ACKNOWLEDGMENTS

For inspiring me to write and in fulfilment of a promise, I wish to express my deepest gratitude to Margaret Kirrane, (MSLETB) Culleens, Meelick, Swinford, Co Mayo. RIP and Beatrice Brophy MSLETB for transcribing the manuscript.

I wish to acknowledge and thank Kathryn Conway, Maura O'Connell, Brenda Ormsby and in particular Patricia Conway for their unselfish time spent in proofreading for errors and copyright compliance.

A big thanks to my loyal friends Seamus Bermingham and Sean Leach for always being there to support, help and encourage me in this long journey.

Thank you to all my friends at the Mayo Genealogy Group who have been a tremendous support.

And finally, I wish to thank Jackie Kelly, MSLETB and our *"Scribes and Scribblers Ink"* Writing Group, for the time spent on the technical support throughout the production of this book.

TABLE OF CONTENTS

DEDICATION iii
ACKNOWLEDGMENTS v
FOREWORD xi

Chapter 1 1
EARLY MEMORIES 1
Family Tree 7
CHAPTER 2 9
VISITORS 9
Chapter 3 17
FRIENDS and NEIGHBOURS 17
Chapter 4 21
CHANGES 21
Chapter 5 25
SORROW 25
Chapter 6 31
SCHOOLDAYS 31
Chapter 7 37
EVENTFUL YEARS 37
Chapter 8 47
A NEW SCHOOL 47

Chapter 9	57
SECONDARY SCHOOL	57
Chapter 10	63
POLITICAL AWARENESS	63
Chapter 11	73
FARMING	73
Chapter 12	77
FCA DAYS	77
Chapter 13	101
ENGLAND	101
Chapter 14	135
FARM DEVELOPMENT	135
Chapter 15	145
LAST DAYS in ALLSCOTT	145
Chapter 16	147
HOME CHANGES	147
Chapter 17	151
FULL TIME FARMING	151

FOREWORD

In rural Ireland our relationship to the land is more than just an economic connection, it is also an emotional one. In the decades following the establishment of the Irish State, entire families left their small farms and emigrated to Britain, America, Canada and Australia. They did so in the vain hope that someday they might return to their homeplace, and in more prosperous times, would enjoy a sustainable and dignified existence back in their own townlands and parishes.

The legacy of that expectation, that vain hope, left a scar across all our townlands. Desolated homesteads became a feature in the rural landscape, testimony to economic failure in post-colonial Ireland. But also, this was in part due to a landlord class, which in the 1830s and 1840s created small unsustainable holdings that would encompass a combination of good and marginal land, thus ensuring that every farm would be capable of yielding some kind of rent. This was regardless of the challenges which then had to be faced by the hard-pressed tenant farmers.

For those who left, their strong emotional ties to the family homestead meant that they were unable to sell their farms, even though they could have used the modest proceeds of such sales to make a fresh start in their new countries of adoption. Instead, they leased their farms at nominal rents to neighbouring landowners in lieu of their houses being maintained, and their property kept in good order until they returned.

In his book "Nineteen Acres", John Healy illustrates the longing for continuity by the last act of the emigrants bringing a coal to their neighbour's fire. The expectation was thus that the family fire would never go out and a live coal from the neighbour`s fire would be brought back, along with the tongs, to the old homestead on their return.

But very few returned, some were never heard of again, those who kept in touch and returned annually would eventually relent and sell their modest farms as they prepared for retirement in their adopted countries.

The world of the small holding is deeply etched into the Irish psyche. In politics one needs to look no further than the Great Irish Famine, or Michael Davitt and the Irish Land League. In literature Heaney, Kavanagh and John B Keane amongst others, transformed the intimacies and dramas of Irish rural life into great works of art.

Martin Neary`s memoir, simply told in his own words, embraces the trials, joys and tribulations of rural life. It is conversational in form and sprinkled with beautiful, understated anecdotes laced with Martin`s wry sense of humour. Martin`s connection to his land is an intimate one. Each field has a name and a personality of its own, woven into a rich tapestry of hedgerows and contours that gave each holding its own unique signature, familiar, and yet surreal.

Every farm had its own narrative, and Martin`s is no different, a mixture of folklore and stories about long dead ancestors and neighbours. This is a culture which is slowly slipping into oblivion as families die out or as farms and townlands succumb to unsustainable mass afforestation which offers nothing in terms of biodiversity. It literally renders that culture into pulp, as investors and pension funds ensure that such holdings will no longer be productive farms.

So, in writing this memoir and by gifting his homestead to the people of our parish, Martin ensures that his story and that of his small holding will not succumb to the agenda of those who know the price of everything and the value of nothing.

As a proud Republican and Socialist, Martin is one of those rare individuals whose words are matched by his deeds. Those of us who know him well were not in the least bit surprised when he announced that he had bequeathed his family farm to our local community. It was so in keeping with the philosophy and values of the Martin Neary we have all come to know and to love.

When Martin is finally laid to rest in the clay of his small holding of land in Madogue, that strong emotional connection, that enduring bond to his beloved homestead and long dead ancestors will become eternal. Surely a fitting reward for a man who has given so much.

Councillor Gerry Murray ~ March 2024

Chapter 1

EARLY MEMORIES

I have been told I should write my memoirs. I don't think they would be of interest to many, but I have been considering in old age how I would like to write an account of the people I knew in my childhood and who have long since passed away. Now that I am writing it seems to bring to mind people who had almost faded from my memory and who will be forgotten if I don't do it now.

I was born on the 12th of August 1943 in Madogue, Charlestown. My father was Martin Neary from Drumshinnagh, Swinford and my mother was Bessie Morley from Madogue. I am told I was baptised in Charlestown, something my father would not have approved of because he was an atheist but at that time there was no other way. The church was in charge of everything. Birth to school, to marriage, to old age, to death. I guess I became aware of place and time in my third year. My first memory was of waking up on a bright sunny morning and becoming aware of my mother, father, aunt and grandmother. I was able to talk and converse at that point so I must have learned to talk before my day-to-day memory began to work.

After that I got to know the dog "Tige" who had a great relationship with my father. They were always together on the land. There were two cats, "Peteen" and "O'Hara". Peteen once belonged to a neighbour, Maggie Haran. When she died, Peteen moved in with us. She had kittens once and I remember my father drowning some of them in a mossy swamp in the bog. He had kept one with Peteen, a very black kitten which my father called "Cauby". When potatoes were roasted on the fire, they were called a cast and the skin got very black and was called a caub. That was how he got his name. When he got older my mother went visiting to her cousins in Cully, over the Sligo border. She brought Cauby and myself with her, and on her way gave the cat to a girl, Winnie Lavin, in Lisloughna.

O'Hara, my father got in the shop in John Devaney`s (Mickie) in Culmore. Why he was named O'Hara I don't know. Peteen disappeared first and then O'Hara. That was while my father was alive. It was my first sense of loss. My first time out was with my mother, to a hay field called The Park. There were men mowing up hay and I think it may have been gathered into a pike, after that I remember oats being stooked and my father moving them to drier ground. I remember oats in different fields. It being unlikely that we would have two fields of oats in the one year, it is possible I am remembering different years.

Also, my aunt Maggie used to take me around the blackberries and play among the brooms which didn't have thorns like the whins and briars. Once I remember being with my grandmother in Nicholas Brennan's house; I only saw my grandmother walking twice in my life. The second time was when my father was building a stack of turf and she walked over to the bog. Another time my father and mother took me to Swinford. It must have been a fair day. We visited my aunt Mary Kate who lived with Cissie Doherty, a dressmaker.

My father had some other business that day, I think it was with Jimmie Groarke who was in the IRA with him. We walked home but I guess I was carried most of the way. I think that was the day my grandmother had a stroke. She was walking in the bog and fell into a small trench. Maggie must have found her. I don't remember anything about it but the next day a tall man in black called to the house. I was afraid of him, but my father got me to shake hands with him. He was Canon Blaine, the Parish Priest of Charlestown. He was called because my grandmother was expected to die. She didn't but was unable to look after herself after that.

Other incidents I remember from that time was one day, it must have been harvest time, my father and mother were weaving a straw rope. He had a hook with the start of the rope in it. He kept winding the hook while she kept feeding the straw onto it at her end. The rope kept getting longer and longer. Eventually when it was time, the rope being long enough, my mother rolled it up into a big ball. I started crying, my father wanted to know why but I wouldn't say. He got mad when he couldn't find out why and they continued making more rope. I had cried because I wanted the rope to remain a long rope. When it was rolled into a ball it was not a rope.

Another time my mother was in town and my father was doing some work around the house. I got hiccups. I told him and he said, "You stole a hundred pounds". I couldn't remember doing it but if he said I did it, I must have done it. I went away shocked, wondering what was going to be done about it. I came back to him after a while and he said, "Are the hiccups gone?" It dawned on me then that I didn't have any since I heard I had stolen the hundred pounds. He explained to me that the way to cure hiccups was to be told a story that would shock you and take your mind off them.

Martin's school photos taken between 1949 and 1956

Martin Neary
12/08/1943
Mullenmadoge
Kilbeagh

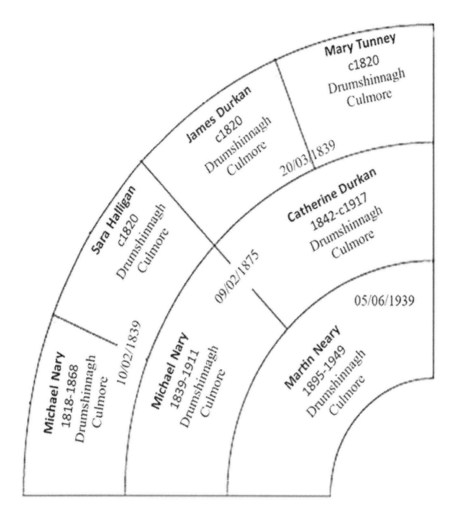

Source: Seamus Bermingham, Charlestown

FATHER'S FAMILY

FAMILY TREE

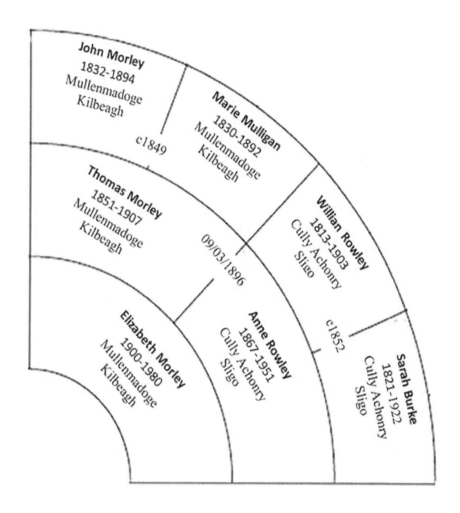

MOTHERS'S FAMILY

CHAPTER 2

VISITORS

After Canon Blaine I remember different visitors to the house. There was a man called Dick Henry who was an engineer. He always had a wide hat and as I grew up, I always recognised him when he passed in his car. Pension officers came but I didn't get their names, they may not have given any. I remember a traveller woman with a coloured shawl and a basket. At times a young fellow from Charlestown, Devaney, used to call selling fish. The fish would be cooked on the fire as would mushrooms which Maggie would collect in the fields. The herrings would be put on a tongs which would be propped up over the fire. The mushrooms would have a little salt put on to them and they were put on hot coals.

Mike Morley called in during the daytime and talked with my father when he was working. Mike was born on our land and the site of his house is still there. Tom Burns was a good friend of my father and helped him with the home jobs. Sometimes he would call when he was hunting. He would leave the gun on the floor and I was very fascinated by it. One day my father and Tom made a wheel for a barrow. Tom's father was a carpenter and blacksmith and I guess Tom was too. Another time my father wanted to put up a mantelpiece in the kitchen. They collected suitable pieces of timber and planed them,

(Tom had the plane), and one night they were putting it together when a crowd of girls called. They were collecting for the Jubilee nurse. There was a house full of people there for a while and there was a lot of laughing and craic. Twenty years after, one of those girls, Mary Morley from Sonnagh, was burnt to death when her house caught fire. The mantelpiece was installed and was painted and lasted while the house was in use.

I remember Matt Devaney (Mackie) calling. He belonged to a well-off family in my father's village, Drumshinnagh, but he decided to go off on his own, wandering the roads in England and Ireland. He may have got the habit when he was in England after WWI and a lot of Irish were over there out of work. They would be employed on farms for the hay, beet and harvest and then they would travel around from town to town looking for more work. Some of them got so used to that sort of life they stayed that way for the rest of their lives. Matt would get meat in a butcher shop, sleep in a shed or barn and would call to a house in the morning and cook his meat. He enjoyed it very much. He would hold it with his teeth and his hand and cut off mouthfuls with the knife. I think he lived into the 60s but was in a home in Castlebar which may have shortened his life.

Kathleen Brennan was another interesting visitor at that time. She was Nicholas Brennan's daughter and had been in London in a place called

Garden City, she was young and stylish. She had a light raincoat, blue in colour, which she left to my mother when she went back. My mother and Kathleen decided to go to O'Neill's pub one night. They had to walk over two miles there and I suppose I had to be carried most of the way. Two cars passed us on the way. Each car blew the horn. That time there would be people wandering about on the road and there were not many cars. The first car beeped and the second car, a bigger one, gave a honking sound. That was of interest to me. Someone talked to me once about a child's sense of wonder and looking back I can see that everything is new to a child and that may be why we remember so much from our childhood.

In O'Neill's we were in the kitchen of the house, but the pub was a separate building. There were six or seven people in the kitchen as well as us, a lot of talk went on. It was a very pleasant house with a big fire and it seemed to be very brightly lit. The only thing I took notice of on the way home was the shrine in Culmore. It was lit up and there were statues standing up inside. I couldn't understand what it was all about. When I got home, Uncle Mick was visiting so I asked him and my father why there were statues standing up in that small little house. Mick explained the whole thing, but I cannot remember the story he told me. It may be because it did not make sense to me. As Mick and my father were atheists, the story would not be relevant. I would have to wait another couple of years and go to school before I would learn anything about shrines or chapels. Kathleen used to go to dances with Mary Burns and everyone was fond of her, but she went back to England and I never saw her again. She is probably long dead now.

Another visitor was Jim Morley, a stepbrother of Kathleen. Her mother was married to Morley first and they had two children, Jim and Mary. She married Nicholas Brennan after, but the land was left to Morley's son Jim. He may have made two visits, but I remember him giving a wooden pipe to my father. He used to use clay pipes. There were plenty of them. They could be found on top of ditches, having been left there after wakes but they were easily broken so the wooden pipe would last longer. Jim cut some turf for his stepfather Nicholas that year and later he sold the land to Tom Mulligan. He made some agreement with him about Nicholas because his stepfather lived with the Mulligans until his death.

Aunt Mary Kate used to visit and the first visit I remember was of great interest because she had all sorts of sweets and buns and stuff like that. She also had books, picture books and comics, a lot of religious books and I remember one very big book. When I learnt to read, I found it was the "Capuchin Annual" for 1946. There was a report and pictures of the funeral of John Count McCormack. There were other stories about Kinsale and pictures of all the most important people in the country at that time. They were also very funny cartoons done by a Fr Gerard. Some of it survives here to the present day but it is almost impossible to turn the pages now.

Mary Kate came again, this time with my uncle Jim and his daughter, who may have been a year older than me. That was a fine sunny day. They came on the bus from Swinford and Jim Burns carried the child on the bike from the stop at the Halfway Bush. We played in the garden and Maureen, (I think that was her name), could walk on her hands. I have never seen anyone do this since. That was the first time I saw tomatoes. I thought they were sweet, but they disappeared and they remained in my mind for days. Jim and my father walked through all the fields. Jim had known them since childhood and pointed out things my father did not know. He called again another evening after that. It was probably to say goodbye to his mother and the rest of us. He may have walked from Swinford because he came across the bog from the main road. Like Kathleen Brennan, I never saw him or his daughter again.

In the night-time there used to be a crowd of young lads in the house. And on Sunday nights Uncle Mick Neary came from Culmore. He was an atheist but that didn't stop him telling ghost stories in which the devil would often feature. A lot of young men would come in and enjoy the craic and they always smoked cigarettes. My mother smoked cigarettes also, but my father, Grandmother and Maggie smoked pipes. Tom McIntyre, Patsy Stenson, Martin Brennan, Tom Burns, Frank Burns, Jimmie, Tom and Henry Peyton would tell their stories and smoke. Sometimes one of them would find part of a bracelet or a plastic wristband (I have it yet) and a broken cigarette lighter and give it to me. I loved getting things and stored them in a shoebox. Once Tom Peyton had a coin about the size of a half crown but there was a hole in the middle of it. Their cousin Jim Morris had been working in India and that was the new Indian money after independence. I enjoyed that time very much.

My mother and I visited Ed Grantham's house a number of times. Their name was Gallagher, but they were called Grantham because their father Jim worked in England, in Grantham. There were so many families of the same name that the way to know them was by their nicknames. It was a sunny day. Days always seemed to be fine then. The three kids, that was all they had at the time, were sent to the well and I went with them. The well was at the end of the land near the river. The spring was strong flowing and the water was very cold.

On the way back, we had to climb hills, go through narrow gaps in fences and to make sure gates were closed. Along the way we rested and played. Jimmie was about three years older than me; Maureen was two years older and Eamon was my age. Myself and their father Ed would have been second cousins. When we got back with the water,

Winnie, their mother was making tea and she gave us the empty sugar bag. However, she made sure to leave some sugar in it and the kids emptied it onto a stool and made four little heaps of sugar, one for each of us. When we were going home that evening, Jimmie gave me a small wooden car the same shape as the old Prefect cars of that time. There was one wheel missing but that made no difference to me. I was very proud of my car for years after.

My father had cut the turf for Winnie while Ed was in England where he used to work for most of the year. More children came along and Tom was born the year of the blizzard, 1947. My father came home and told us that he was not the size of a football. He later became my lifelong friend. Later that year they moved from Madogue to Culmore to Winnie's home place. Their mare Molly pulled the cart and took all their stuff to the new house. I can still see the cart going down the road.

One other occasion I remember was my aunt Eileen's visit from America. She and John Dooner called one day to our house. They had a bottle of whiskey with them and everyone had drinks. Some days later Lena McNulty, cousin Matt's wife, called to say they were having a party in Aunt Agnes' house and we were invited. My father, mother and I walked to the house in Drumshinnagh, which was about a mile and a half away. I remember there was a gypsy caravan parked at the head of the Madogue road. It was the first time I had seen one of these caravans and my child's sense of wonder was very strong. At the party the house was full of people, the two musicians were Mary Ann Gallagher Neary and Mary Dillon Horkan. Mary Anne played the accordion and also sang. I remember one song "The Ship That Never Returned ", and another one, "Barbara Allen". Mary Dillon played the fiddle. A lot of people sang, and one was Anthony Byrne who was reared in Ann Sheerin's house next door. Another tall, good-looking, very impressive man give a recitation. I remembered some of the words for years afterwards but sadly not now. I was told he was Tom Horkan. About that time, Tom would have come home from England and bought Parsons` shop and land at Culmore school. He is dead now. He was a great character who was liked by everybody.

I don't remember anything more about Aunt Eileen or her husband going back to America. I think John Donner was a Roscommon man, and they may have had a pub or saloon in Philadelphia. Tommy Durcan told me a story once that Eileen was very good looking and attracted a lot of boys. One of them came from Killaturley, Paddy Fatch Mhor. About that time young lads would have to wear a dress until they were twelve or more or until they could afford a trousers. (This had changed by the 20s). She ignored him and had no time for him. They both emigrated to America, she arrived in Philadelphia, and Paddy Fatch Mhor joined the army. He found out where she was living, called to her house and showed her his fine new army trousers.

Chapter 3

FRIENDS and NEIGHBOURS

There were quite a number of old people in the village at the time. The men were: Pat Gallagher, Navvy Mulligan, James Mulligan, Nicholas Brennan and Mike Morley. The women were: Eileen Gallagher nee Doherty, wife of Pat; Beezie Mulligan nee Dillon wife of Navvy Mulligan; Maggie Mulligan, better known as "Yankee", widow of John Mulligan; Agnes Peyton, widow of Bar Peyton, (known as Bar because he had been reared in Barroe, Carracastle); Anne Rowley, my grandmother; Kate Gallagher nee Mannion, widow of John Gallagher (known as "Shopboy"); Maggie Gallagher nee Conway, widow of Jim Grantham; Bridget Durcan nee Gallagher, widow of Paddy Durcan.

Pat Gallagher had travelled quite a bit. He had been to Alaska and may have been to Russia. Nicholas Brennan had been to America and worked for Wells Fargo on the railways for years. He had a different way of cooking. The others had all worked for years in England. I knew Mike Morley best.

Eileen Gallagher had lived in the village all her life. She had a sister Anne who worked as a milliner in Swinford. Beezie Dillon was from Lurga. Maggie "Yankee" was a stooped, hard-working woman from Killaturley. She was very intelligent and had books from before her father's time. He used to read them at wakes and funerals, as at that time there were not many priests about and they would only attend the most important occasions. She said at one time, she and her sister told him to stop doing it as the priests were taking over. One of the books she had was in Irish and as she was reading it the Curate Higgins called and when he saw the book, he said, "Will you leave me this book when you die?". She said, "I will give it to you now Father". I wonder what happened to it.

Agnes Bar Peyton nee Callaghan was from Cloonagh, County Sligo. She had been married before in America and had a daughter, Anna McMahon. She had met Bar over there. He had also been married before, to a Regan from Stripe and also had family with her. Agnes and Bar had family as well. One of the daughters died of TB and a son was killed in a subway in New York. I think Tom Peyton told me that Agnes used to say she always put on fresh underwear going to town in case she had an accident.

My grandmother, Anne Rowley, came from Cully in Sligo and I knew very little about her as she suffered from a stroke in my time.

Kate Gallagher's husband John, "Shopboy", may have been delicate because he used to eat town bread. When Kate would invite someone in for tea she would say, "Come in and I will give you a piece of John's loaf". She was a good manager and had everything in order. She was from Barnacogue and had a brother who became a priest. She had a special room which had a boarded floor, a wardrobe, a sideboard, a washstand and a table lamp with a coloured globe. This room was for the priest if he called. Kate's grandniece, Maggie O'Brien, came to live with her, married and became the grandmother of Noel and Liam Gallagher of the famous band Oasis.

Maggie Gallagher nee Conway, was from the same village as my grandmother, Cully, County Sligo. She was also a very good manager and other women would ask her advice on household things. The making of butter was one, at times of the year it could be very white, and shopkeepers would prefer a gold colour. Maggie knew the answer to all of those problems. It was a famous house for poitin making and Maggie had to entertain the customers.

Bridget Durcan nee Gallagher from Culmore was married to Paddy Durcan, a good farmer. He grew beet. My first memory of walking the road was to see stacks of beet piled along the road waiting for the lorry to take them to the factory. Paddy Durcan was the second man in the village to get a bicycle. Bridget's favourite swear word was "Good Christ". It could be mistaken for a prayer, but it wasn't.

Chapter 4

CHANGES

After that most memories are to do with work. My father had applied for a grant to build a fence. The new fence would run by an old one-roomed house with a small garden and two little sheds where pigs and chickens were kept. I knew it as Pegeen Owen's house. She was Gallagher and she married John McNulty of Killasser who may have been a farm labourer. They were married in the 1870s and had five or six children. Pegeen would have died in the 1920s. As he dug around the house my father dug up a lot of stuff like handles of buckets, glass jars, crockery including broken plates and jugs with beautiful paintings of colourful flowers, and also old clay pipes and one or two whiskey glasses. On fine days I loved collecting all the old stuff and arranging it as a shop.

I think my father would get £7 of a grant. He had to mark out the space first, with two narrow tracks on each side of the fence. The fence was to be part of a new field, some of which would contain some already arable land but more of it would be land growing heather off which turf was harvested years before. There was also at least half an acre of very wet ground which my father was planning to drain.

Eileen, who lived on the other side of our place, used to cross this field when going to the well or to town. My father expected her to walk along the fence, but she refused to do so, insisting on crossing the field at an angle. This made it very awkward for ploughing as the plough had to be lifted every time it crossed her path. He also had to put in two extra gates where the path crossed the fence. The building of the fence continued for some time and when it was finished, a man came one day and inspected it and after that my father got the grant.

Ellen Smith also had a road running through our land. It didn't go in the direction of the well or the town road, but it was the legal way out. At one spot along the road there was a lake and it used to flood the road from time to time. Tom Burns used to be a good friend of Ellen and he asked my father could he dig some soak holes to drain the water. My father agreed and Tom dug about seven soak holes into loose gravel. They drank up the water and lowered the level of the lake and left the road dry after that. Tom got £7 for that from Ellen, the same as my father got for the fence. I remember at that time Mike Morley would spend a lot of time talking to my father. He explained he was born about twenty yards from where my father was working. He showed the outline of a road and a garden, a lime kiln and the trace of a house and barn. I've always called that field Mike's garden.

In the spring Willie Morley ploughed a section of the field and used the horse and cart to put out the top dress. My father set potatoes on most of the ploughed section, but he also set turnips, onions and cabbage plants. I remember later in the year a young lad from Corthoon, Tom Morley, collecting plants which may have been sold or gifted by my father. As the year went by, the "mowling" (moulding/earthing up) had to be done twice followed by the spraying with blue stone. Willie Morley's big timber barrel was used. Paddy McGrath had borrowed it, so we had to go to his house to collect it. It was filled with water and a small bag of blue stone was left hanging in the water off a rail at the top of the barrel. It was left there overnight. In the morning the water had turned a sort of greenish colour. Washing soda had to be added to the spray. That was put into a can of hot water and dissolved. Then it was poured into the barrel. The colour of the spray changed to a very strong blue at first - just in the spot where it was poured - but then as it was being mixed it spread and took over the whole barrel. To me it was a strange, fascinating sight. After that my father and mother filled buckets of spray and used freshly made besoms of heather to shake the spray onto every potato stalk in the field. This had to be done twice at least and was unpleasant because when the stalks got higher and broader it could involve getting very wet.

I have no memory of the digging of the potatoes at the time or it may have faded from my memory. However, I do remember the turnips being fed to the cows in the winter. They were chopped into a trough and the cows seemed to enjoy them very much. I also remember my father selling hay in the winter. There were two big pikes of hay in the field at the barn near Haran`s house. Early in that summer I remember Tom Shiel from Meelick and Tom Mulligan helping to build them. He must have used Willie's donkey and cart to bring the hay to the market, and I cannot remember who helped him load it. It may have been Tom Burns.

The following year was a repeat of the year before. My father had a second section of the fields ploughed by Willie. Oats was set in the first section. The second one was harder than before. Part of it grew heather and had never been ploughed before and my father had to turn it by hand. A third section was wet and also had to be turned by hand. The field would have to be drained if it was to be used the following year. When trimming a fence known as "John`s fence" he had found a place where an attempt had been made to drain the wet part into a sandpit of loose gravel. He planned to do that the following winter.

Chapter 5

SORROW

The year wore on until about July. My father was at the turf one day when he got a pain and felt weak. He used to suffer from arthritis (or "new rites" as he called it) when in America. He became weaker and couldn't do much.

After some time, my aunt Mary Kate got him into the hospital in Swinford for a fortnight. When he came out he was no better. In time he decided to get a doctor. The Morleys' doctor was Dr Cawley in Swinford. He was a young man at the time. He examined my father and told the Morleys that his problem was the heart. When they told my father, he didn't believe it. He said Dr Cawley was young and wouldn't know as much as an older doctor. He insisted on getting Dr Byrne from Charlestown who was an older man. However, Dr Byrne confirmed that the heart was the problem. He was depressed after that period. The doctors said that with the condition one could live for forty years or die in a minute. The winter wore on, my aunts would come at weekends and cook things they thought were good for him. People would come to see him. I remember Tom Shiel at one time. He went to bed more often and had to be helped there and back by my mother. There was no fun or jokes with the young crowd anymore. At some point he had a lawyer out and some arrangement was made. The winter turned to spring and I guess that would have made him feel worse. In late May, Willie Morley and Tom Burns decided to cut a bank of turf for my mother. It was a beautiful sunny day and they came early. It was the highest bank in the land with about ten spits in part of it. I had been watching them working and when I came in, my father who was on his way to bed, being helped by my mother, collapsed on the floor.

She told me to call the men and this I did. Willie and Tom came at once and they got him into bed. He was still able to talk because I could hear him calling my mother pretty often. After that it became quiet. The priest came but I did not see him. People started coming in, one of them was Tommy Neary, my father's nephew. I was put to bed and before I went to sleep I could hear loud talking and words being repeated all the time. I discovered afterwards they were saying the Rosary. I had never heard it before. I had never heard anyone praying in the house until that night. If my father was able the priest would not have been sent for either.

In the morning I was woken by my mother and she told me my father was dead. At that age, five, I guess one just accepts things, like summer follows the winter and bad weather follows good weather. I had to go along with it. In the years that followed, and all through my life, I have realised what a huge loss he was. In my everyday living and in the field of education and confidence I had to learn things at school and at home, which others of my age would know before they left their own home.

The following couple of days went by with a lot of things happening. A coffin was brought to the house and my father was put into it. The lid was left standing against the wall. There was a wake, but I have no memory of it. The following morning in the room, I saw cigarettes, cut up tobacco and a bottle of rum. I must have been given a taste of the rum because I always wanted to drink it after that. A lot of people called during the day. One person from the town, Jimmy McCarthy, was there. The only other place I would have seen him was in his shop in Charlestown. In the evening, when they were going to bring my father to Bushfield Church, Mike Ginty, another nephew, took me into the house where I saw them putting on the lid on the coffin and Luke Mulligan screwing down the nails. It was carried out to the hearse on the road. There was a lot of people walking behind but Luke told my mother and myself to get in the hearse so that is how we got to Bushfield.

It was my first time on that road, and everything was new to me. The wall on the right side of Trout Hill Bridge had been knocked into the river. It may have been hit by a truck. From the bridge and for some distance up the Quarry Road running along the river was land owned by Dominic Harrison. This had never been fenced. Generations of the Ward family used to camp there, and their children were born there, some of whom I knew in later years. Another bridge we passed on our way was known as the Red Bridge because red brick was used in the building of it. We arrived at Bushfield Church and the coffin was carried in. It was my first time in a church, there was no talking and people at different times would stand up, then sit down and then kneel down. One could see their mouths moving so I figured they were praying. I cannot remember how we got home. We may have walked.

The following morning, I think we had a car which was organised by Aunt Mary Kate. There was a crowd in the church and then the coffin was taken to the graveyard. I remember men carrying it to the graveyard. The grave was at the end and was the last one in the line on the right. I recall a pile of earth, sand and stones. There were more prayers and then the coffin was lowered into the grave. More prayer started again, and Harry Peyton had to tap Mick Neary on the shoulder to stop him working. After that, the grave was filled in by Bill Sweeney and Mick and there may have been others. I could hear the stones landing on the coffin at the beginning. As it filled up it was quiet and when they were finished there was a mound about 6 inches higher than the ground. The diggers tidied the raised area which was the length of the coffin and three feet wide. They slapped it down smooth with their shovels and left some stones on top in the shape of a cross. On our way home in the car, it could have been that day or the evening before, we went down the Bushfield road to Charlestown and we me a big man driving cattle. My mother said he was Melter Gallagher. He may have died shortly after because I never saw him again, but I got to know his son Tom, with whom I would be friends in Charlestown for many years after.

After my father's death, life continued but not at the same pace as when my father was there. He always had a plan and was always doing something new. Now nothing happened. Bill Sweeney cut a bank of turf for my mother. Willie Morley looked after all the hay, potatoes and oats. There were two cows and their calves on the land at the time and Willie used to graze the rest of the land. There were thirty-six acres and seventeen perches but there were only about seven acres of green grassy land. Most of the land was growing heather or wild grass on fields that had been green in the past. There had been no man on the place from when my grandfather died in 1907 until my father came there in 1939. It had now returned to that situation again.

Chapter 6

SCHOOLDAYS

I must have started school in the summer of 1950. The Morleys (Michael John and Tony) brought me there on a sunny summer morning. We went the long way, on to the main road first and then on to Corthoon. Later we crossed the fields by McIntyres, a way which was much shorter. When I arrived in school there was a big crowd of kids there of different ages. I was put with Frank Peyton my neighbour, Brian Donohue, Angela Mulligan and Margaret Mulligan. In later years we were joined by Chris Brett and Mary Margaret Corley from other classes. The teacher was Frances Walsh who I thought was a lovely person. She was replacing Mrs. Cassidy who was the regular teacher but was off sick. Frances didn't continue teaching but ran a shop with her brother in Charlestown. When plays were staged in Charlestown she was always a leading member of the cast. I got to know my classmates, in particular Frank, who was great fun and continued this way throughout his life. I also got to know the other kids who looked to me as grown men and women.

On the boys' side there were the Cassidy twins, Cathal and Louis, and Billy Morley, Henry Peyton, Jerry Walsh, Jack Foley, Pete Morley and Paddy Duffy. On the female side there were Mary Mulligan and her twin sisters Margaret and Kathleen, Teresa Morley, Patricia

Donoghue, Marian Goldrick, Eileen McIntyre, Frances Duffy and Kathleen Brett. There were two yards or playgrounds, one for boys and the other for girls. The big boys played football and rounders which was a game where there was a home station and three outlying stations. One team was at home and the other was out. The out team had to knock the home team out. To do this, the ball was tossed to a member of the home team by one of the outs. The home guy tossed the ball into the yard and ran to the first station. If one of the out team caught the ball and hit him before he reached the station he was out and so it went on.

The small boys played at the front and had to make up their own games. The girls didn't seem to have any particular game and we never knew what they did because the separation of the sexes was strictly maintained. School finished at two for infants and at three for older kids. I had to wait for the Morleys and Sean Harrington in High Infants had to wait for his brother Eugene. Both of us were allowed to play in the yard until three o`clock. Sean was a cousin of mine but we didn't know that at the time. He was a nice friendly lad and we got on very well. In later life he went on to become a priest in the foreign missions in the Philippine Islands. After some years, he got laicised, came back to London, got married and had a family. He died young. I miss him for whenever he came on holidays we had long talks. Mrs. Cassidy was back after the summer holidays, I was learning reading and writing in Irish and English, and maths which in later life I did not like. We made things with plasticine, soft rubber stuff which one could twist and bend. We also did some drawing. However, the big surprise for me was religion. In my father's time I had heard nothing at all about religion and all the people who came to the house never talked about it.

Hell was a swear word and the devil was talked about a lot by my uncle when he was telling ghost stories, but my father said not to believe them. A lot of the day in school was used for catechism, a new word for me. It was very unpleasant but seeing that the teachers and priests and shopkeepers said it was true I believed it. Nobody disagreed with them except my uncle Mick and everyone said he was a liar. This was a new kind of storytelling. There was a God with three heads, and he was all powerful. He knew what everyone was saying and doing. He lived up in heaven. He was good. The devil was bad, he lived in hell. The world would end. There would be a last day which could happen anytime.

The good people would go to Heaven and the gates would close. The bad people would go to hell. Mrs. Cassidy knew what hell was like. It was a big fire and all the bad people would burn there forever and ever. She didn't know what heaven was like. She said it would be a bright place and you would be happy sitting there looking at God all the time. After learning how to be good I knew that all my friends and people I liked were going to go to hell. Only the priest Fr Kirwan, the teachers, some well-dressed shopkeepers, and the old parish priest Fr O'Hara had a chance of going to heaven. But this didn't seem altogether likely because he used to stand at the altar at Sunday Mass and start shouting and jumping around. I had heard the guards in Charlestown (there were about eight of them) were very heavy drinkers so they hadn`t a hope. I didn't have much of a chance either. I didn't want to go to hell and burn forever but going to heaven and sitting watching God forever would not be much fun either, so I thought the best chance I had was to get good before I died and keep out of the fire.

When I was at home at night there were no kids in the house. It was very lonely, so I thought about being in heaven a lot. Fr Kirwan would be in charge and there would be no fun wherever he was. My father would have made a joke of the whole thing but now everyone was a believer. They went to mass every Sunday and my mother started saying the rosary. They had to be right and so I was brain washed for the next fifteen years. 1950 went on slowly. I got used to school. Frank was my friend and we played a lot together.

I also mixed a lot with the Sweeney kids. There were eight of them at the time. There were two lads, Paddy and John, who are older than me, and the girls Bridie, Peggy, Kathleen, Nell, Ann and Una who was a baby. I often saw the Gallaghers, my cousins, who had moved to Culmore. I mixed with the McIntyres in Corthoon, Angela and Brendan who was my age, and the Morleys. I saw them most days as they were minding their cattle on my land.

Chapter 7

EVENTFUL YEARS

Going into 1951, my grandmother, Anne Rowley got bad and as time went on, got worse. Aunt Mary Kate was coming to see her regularly and Tommy Neary used to help out a lot and so did Maggie Sweeney. One day the priest, Fr Gavaghan, came out and did what he had to do. I remember sometime before that stations would be held in the school twice a year. Everyone went there and had mass and confessions. After the stations were over the priest visited the old people who were sick or couldn't go there. Fr Kirwan was still in Charlestown and he came to see my grandmother. Nicholas Brennan was also there. My grandmother, who had suffered a stroke some years before, would not be aware of what was happening, but Nicholas was well aware.

He had spent several years in America and worked for Wells Fargo on the railroads and didn't practise religion except when he was forced to. Fr Kirwan got him to say the Confiteor, something which had the words "through my fault" repeated three times. Nicholas said it once, but Fr Kirwan was a stickler for protocol and kept pushing him to say, "through my fault" three times. Nicholas put a stop to that by saying "God damn it, Yes, Yes, Yes". Fr Kirwan thought it better to give up.

After eighteen years in Charlestown Kirwan had been transferred to some other parish and he had been replaced by two younger priests when my grandmother got bad. She went on being in bed and having trouble breathing and being turned from time to time by my mother, my aunt who was there all the time now, Maggie Sweeney and Tommy Neary. One night the breathing seemed to get worse. They kept trying to change her position to make her more comfortable, but it didn't do any good. Near the morning she gave a big breath, opening and then closing her mouth. That happened twice more, then she went very still.

Everyone there came to the conclusion that she was dead. Her mouth was very wide open. After a while they got a length of cloth and tied it tightly around the lower jaw and the head. This closed the mouth and it was taken off after some time. In the morning, my mother and Tommy went to town and ordered a coffin. They must have got a car, probably that of John Thomas Durcan. Luke Mulligan arrived with the coffin later in the day. There was a wake which I don't remember everything of now and the funeral was the same as my father's two years before.

Bill Sweeney and Mick Neary dug the grave and filled it in. This time I remember a niece of my grandmother and first cousin of my mother, Annie Rowley (Mrs. Farrell) being there and helping around the place.

Life continued and the next issue was with my First Communion. It seems that I had missed school at that time, and it was felt I wouldn't be fit for the examination. My mother may have insisted I be included. The priest who carried out the examination was Fr Flannery who had a sister a nun in Swinford years afterwards. The question he put to me was: "What was the difference between angels and people?" I said we had bodies and they hadn't. He asked the next lad how God would get in the Host. He said he would fly down. I thought that was the right answer. However, the new teacher, Evelyn Mullarkey, who was replacing Mrs. Cassidy again, praised me for my answer but gave out strongly to the other lad for saying God would fly to the Host. She said, "It's a wonder you didn't say he would take a plane". We had a list of sins put together and had learned them off by heart. When the priest, Fr Henry, came we were well prepared, and it passed off with no trouble. I had got a new suit and on Sunday in Bushfield, I received with a seat full of other kids. I noted that most of them had white shirts on, but I wore my jacket. My aunt in Swinford was impressed and give me a [Rosary] beads in a little case with a picture of the Pope on it. She said it was blessed in Rome by the Pope himself.

Another trouble involved my Aunt Maggie at home. She had lived there all her life. She had not been to school much and would have been a slow learner or perhaps there is a better term for it. One day she just got blind. Years afterwards it happened to my mother also, but slowly. She was diagnosed with glaucoma. In Maggie's time it appeared little was known and little could be done about it. My mother took her to the doctor in Charlestown. I think Mick Lenehan drove her there in his car. She had never been in a car before and was very frightened. Dr Laffey examined her and said she had cataracts. All that could be done was to give her a blind pension which she got in the end. In the 60s she also got a radio. She had to be led about the place, and this my mother would do if she was doing anything at the hay or in the bog.

Sometimes my mother and Maggie Sweeney used to visit McIntyres, Mary Feeley or Corley's Shop. There were six or seven kids down there and I used to mix with them. In long winter nights the roads were often frozen and in shaded spots we would have long slides. Sometimes Chris Brett would make his own slide by splashing water on the road and by night-time it would become a sheet of ice. The slide used to go on for hours when my mother and Maggie went into Mary Feeley. Mary had a big court case coming up. She had sold her land and had excluded her son Martin from the will. It appears that Martin had been in America and had come home and built a dance hall called Feeley`s Hall. It did very well for a time, but it had to close in the end and there were some debts. Martin had to go to England and the parents blamed him for getting the place into debt. The mother sold the place to Tom O`Brien in Bushfield. Then she changed her mind. Her brother Michael put an SOS on Radio Eireann for Martin. She tried to get the land back, to buy it at first and when the buyer wouldn't sell, she decided to go to law. Her lawyer, Kelly, wouldn't work for her, so she got one in Castlebar - Mick Moran, a Fianna Fail TD. The case went on for a number of years and was adjourned from time to time. My mother and Maggie used to visit Corley's Shop at the time and then would call to Mary. Her husband had died about a year before that and she liked visitors. Kids were always there - McIntyres, Corleys from the shop and others. A girl from Moran's office called once a week to Mary and to Corley's Shop. She gave the Corley kids a pup and when they got tired of him they gave him to me. His name was Brownie, a small little dog which I had for many years after. Moran's secretary was Josie Staunton from Bohola. She used to have great news and stories from Bohola. They had a fine camogie team and clubs for different things and a very cranky parish priest.

Many nights were spent discussing the case. On the day of the court case when I was going to school, I saw Josie Staunton loading all the people involved into a car. However, after a long day in court the case was adjourned. Talking afterwards about the case it was felt that Mary was going to win. However, when the case came up again it was lost. It was appealed again and lost again. If you sell something and get paid for it and then try to get it back when the buyer doesn't want to give it back, there isn't much that can be done. Mary died some years afterwards, and her son Martin died some years later. Old Michael Corley, the founder of the shop, died. His daughter-in-law Bea (nee

Regan) also died, at a very young age. The shop was closed. Her husband Mike lived on but after his death the place was sold. The children had grown up and gone to England. Of the children, Kathleen and Mike are dead, and the youngest daughter Mary Margaret is in England. The house has not been lived in for years. In its time it was a beautiful house.

It was well designed. The attic had been converted into bedrooms. There were two skylights on the roof. The kitchen was very cosy with a big fire. The wallpaper was red with a design running through it which made the room seem warm. Old Michael had a radio which would be put on for the news. He was a strong Fianna Fail man and no one would dare criticise DeValera. When he was building the house, he insisted on putting in an outshot so he could sleep in the kitchen. They were very busy farmers, had a lot of hens, geese, turkeys, two sows, horses, a trap and lots of machinery that could be used with horses or hand operated. The place was a hive of activity.

The house is still standing but dilapidated. Lots of new houses have been built between Swinford and Charlestown over the years but Corley's Shop is still the most impressive to me. Perhaps it's because I know the history of the place and of the people, most of whom are now long dead, but were a mighty force in their time.

Those were pleasant years for me. I was moving up classes in school and I moved from Mrs. Cassidy's room to her husband's room. He was Pat Cassidy. He was a very nice man, he seemed to like singing. When we were in Mrs. Cassidy's room we had to go out to him for singing lessons. One of the songs he liked to sing was "Beidh aonach amarach i gContae an Chlair". (There will be a fair tomorrow in County Clare).

When we went into third class he said we would have to be examined in order to pass. He gave us a composition to write about a rabbit. I hadn't a clue what a composition was. Other kids knew because they were members of big families and would have seen the older kids do it. I sat there watching Frank Peyton. He wrote a line and I copied it. He complained but I got the gist, and ended my story about a rabbit I knew. It was about a month before the summer holidays and we enjoyed our time there until the last day. It was very quiet, and Pat Cassidy did nothing all day except sit and think. At the end of the day he made a short speech on how he taught so many children in his time and had also taught their parents. He wished us well and said, "You can go now". We rushed out the door and that was that. No goodbyes, after a lifetime. The Cassidys were well into old age. They were supposed to be good teachers. I had only experience of Mrs. Cassidy and thought she was a very good teacher of Irish and of English also. I enjoyed those subjects. I hated maths, not so much then but in later years.

When we went back after the holidays there was a new teacher, Paddy Merriman. He had been four years in Barnacogue school. He was very regular with classes, he was a good teacher at getting things done and maintaining control.

There was a very small yard in Corthoon, there was no green area except on the girls' side. Merriman decided to introduce rugby as the game for lunch break. We got a field off Jim Colleran who was in England and who may not have known that he had given it. We got an oval ball and we learned the rules of rugby. We had been playing it in Colleran's garden first, but the garden got dug up with so many kids jumping on it and so on a very fine summer's day at lunch break we raced up to Colleran's land until we came to a very big field. I remember there was a fort in the field as well. We put down markers and set up goal posts. I don't know how teams were picked but Merriman had a way of doing it, so we had our teams and started playing. He had lunch first and then had trouble finding us. He was afraid it was too far away from the school but that day we played much longer than the lunch break, I don't think we ever played there again as it may have been too far from the school and there may have been trouble with Jim Colleran when he found out we were playing there.

The rugby continued for a while longer, but it came to a stop after I had left Corthoon. I think the priests didn't want it taking over from the GAA. I noted that Merriman didn't teach Christian Doctrine. Fr Higgins would come to the school once a week and talk for an hour.

At that time getting slapped was the done thing. I didn't have any problem with that as one was used to getting a few slaps everyday anyway. There were kids who did their home lessons and were good in school. Often those kids had parents who were themselves intelligent and well-read and showed an interest in their kids' schooling. Teachers worked with those kids and many of them were sent on for scholarships. Most parents were just glad to send their kids off to school and glad to see them come home and go to work footing turf and picking potatoes and all the other jobs that kids had to do in those times. There was little interest taken in the slow learner and there would always be one or two in every class.

Chapter 8

A New School

My mother used to let the land every year, not for grazing as we had two cows and one or two calves, but for conacre. One field called "The Park" was a square field with good soil suitable for ploughing. A person could have a field of potatoes one year and a field of oats the next. However, she had a habit of falling out with people. The first year Willie Morley had it, something went wrong. The next year Tommy Neary had it, something went wrong there too. After that Corleys from the shop had it for two years. The last year it was seeded as four years was the time a field was used for root crops, then the field would be rested by seeding it and growing hay. My mother got some shop seed and two bags of seed from Jimmie Turner (Gallagher) who owned the shop where we used to deal in Charlestown.

In earlier times, Jimmie used to deal in cattle and still had cows and used to sell to local people in the town. His cows would be tied in the shed in winter and where the hay would be fed to them a lot of seed would build up and Jimmie bagged it and gave it to my mother. That was the last time the land was let. Over the years, before my mother got married, she and her mother used to let the land and I think Anne Rowley was easy going and could become a victim of smart dealers and then when they started building the house in 1932 a lot of the stuff disappeared. The contractor was a very unreliable man who tried to get money once he had started the house and if he had got the money he would never have finished it. It was finished in the late thirties and I had receipts from Isaac Beckett, who provided the building material, for many years but now have lost them. When my father came into the place, he took responsibility for everything but now it had gone back to the old ways. My father would have no problem deciding what to do in whatever situation that arose.

My mother was going back to the old ways as in her mother's time. She was expecting the same trouble again. However, in the early fifties the people she was dealing with were not as bad as the ones in the thirties. They would try to get something a little bit cheaper but other than that they were not too bad. However, she fell out with some of those people and the fact that they had kids going to school with me made a problem for me. Some of those kids were not speaking to me either and in that way, life became very unpleasant for me in school. One year after the Christmas holidays I didn't go back the first week and it was harder to go back the next week and after that it became impossible. The priest complained and the guards complained and threatened, and I think summoned my mother in the end. I agreed to go to Culmore school.

I didn't go the day my mother was in court because I was going to make a run for it if anyone came to take me away. It appears I got off, so I went over to Culmore the next day and remained there until the Primary Cert.

My father had decided I would go to Culmore school but when he died there was no one to arrange my going there and it was a much easier option to send me to Corthoon. My father had gone to Culmore and I suppose he wanted me to grow up with the Culmore kids and be part of that new generation of Devaneys and Durcans and Stensons and Horkans and Sheerans and of course there were other villages like Killaturley, Cloonaghboy and Cloonlara. My father's village was Drumshinnagh but it was known as Culmore as well. The only lad I knew in Culmore was Tony Ferguson. He had been fostered by my cousin Tommy Neary. I had some vague knowledge of the two Fenlon families, Martin was Mike's son and Francie was Joe's son. After a short while, I got to know them very well and became good friends with all of them. As well as the Fenlons I got to know three lads from Killaturley: Martin Gallagher, Tommy Gallagher and Seamus Taylor.

Almost everyone in Killaturly was called Gallagher. They had to go by nicknames to know who they were. Martin was known as "Onnie" because that was his grandmother's name. Tommy was known as

"Darkie" and that name may have gone far back in time as there were now two families using that name. Seamus didn't have to change his name as he was the only Taylor in Killaturly. Jack Pidgeon came from Cloonaghboy, so did Martin Sheeran and Jimmie Gallagher. Classes changed and moved into the Master's room. New classmates included Kevin Stenson, Charlie Gallagher, Tom and Tony Pidgeon, Joe McDermott, Martin McNicholas and a lot of others. There were no girls in my class. I think the class was too big, so they were kept back to a lower class.

Martin James Cassidy was the head teacher and Mai McEvaddy taught the younger kids. Martin James was a friendly jokey sort of man who could tell good stories. When he wasn't teaching, he was a member of Mayo County Council. People used to call at lunchtime looking for favours concerning flooding rivers, potholed roads and bog drains. Other times the old people going for their pensions would miss the bus and Martin James would have to take them to town after school. All sorts of visitors used to call. Some were former pupils who had been away in America for years and they would try to identify some of the pupils as the children of their childhood friends. They would leave money and Martin James would get sweets and biscuits the next day. I remember once my cousin Mick Neary called. He was a contractor in England and well off. He left us money. It was a bigger sum than usual and Martin James decided to use it to set up a boys' band. Females seemed to be excluded from everything in those times.

We had great fun with the band in the years that followed. We had to learn how to play the tin whistle. Martin James knew how to play every musical instrument except the Jew's harp and they didn't use that in bands. We learned, some better than others.

I learnt only one tune, `The Dawning of the Day`. Others who liked music could play up to four tunes - `The Wearing of the Green`, `Kelly the Boy from Killane`, and others. Michael McNicholas was the leader of the band in most ways. He could play the drum and organise outings. We got uniforms, first jackets and caps which we collected for. Then we got white trousers which we also collected for. The cloth was bought and the tailor in Swinford, Mick Swords, made them up for us so we had to be measured. That took time and we had great fun doing those things and training on Sunday evenings. We also went to musical gatherings.

One was held in Callow where there was a stage and dancing and singing competitions were held. We played and marched and I heard one man in the crowd say we were well trained! It was a beautiful day. We had tea, sandwiches, ice cream and buns. There were boats in the lake fishing and I remember one of the fishermen was Brendan Howley from Swinford. I think most of us had never seen a real boat being used on water before. As the day wore on we explored the hills around the lakes. We tried to reach the high points but it was difficult and there was long heather, higher than we were, in many places. At the shore of the lake, there was high growing vegetation which I hadn't seen before. There were two or three small lakes on my land but only rushes and moss grew around them. In the evening we came home in two cars, one was Martin James' and the other car was driven by a young man whom I didn't know and will never know now. That was the first time most of us had travelled any further than Swinford or Charlestown.

We also went to sports days in Swinford at Brabazon Park and in Higgins` field in Culmore where they were fundraising for the Culmore football team. Sports days were good days for us. At Brabazon Park there were inter-school football matches. Culmore and Kinaffe, Brackloon, Meelick, Cashel, Tumgesh and Swinford were involved. Swinford would always win. In the sports section there were a lot of races and relay races, high jumps, long jumps and a lot of other events. I came first in the high jump. The first prize for the high jump was a holy picture which, looking back on it, was of no value. I came second in the long jump. The prize for the long jump was a jigsaw which one could enjoy putting together from time to time. I didn't do so well in the running. I was quite good but there were better runners than me.

Another big day in the school was when the stations would be held. Martin James would look after the priests well. I remember there was a priest called Fr McGarry who used to come to the school regularly and he seemed to be a nice man. One year a neighbour called Mag Byrne, I think her right name was Devaney, decided to have the stations in her house. Martin James was very disappointed but he insisted on having the usual party afterwards and we had sweets and biscuits and the rest of the day off. Apart from Martin James, another teacher, PJ Campbell, used to help at times. He was retired from Kinaffe school where he had been principal. He taught Irish to us and was very good. He was known as Pa Jack in the school yard. Most teachers had names which they were called behind their backs. Sometimes Martin J would be off because of his work at the council and at elections and he had been off sick a couple of times.

The thing that used to upset Martin J very much was if something happened of a scandalous nature, a dirty word or a drawing on a copy showing an animal doing something it shouldn't be doing or anything of a sexual nature would set him off on a lecture that would last half the day. He would say he would have to see his confessor and the lecture would continue again the next day when he would give his confessor's opinion on the subject. Some of the older female pupils became aware that whenever a problem like that arose they would get a long break, so they engineered occasions when they would set up something like blaming a younger child for saying something or doing something which they may not have said or done at all. They would get their break and one could see they enjoyed their power to influence events for their own benefit. Male kids of that age would never think of doing that sort of thing.

When Pa Jack was teaching he was very determined to get his lesson across to the pupils and would stay with it until he was sure they had a good grasp of what he had taught. However, one day one of the female pupils decided she needed a break so sitting in a stooped position over a book on a low stool she made a complaint. "Please Sir, so and so rose up my clothes". Pa Jack's cane whistled through the air and he landed three heavy blows on her back, then he continued with the lesson as normal. I am not a sadist, but the sound of the blows landing gave me much pleasure, she learned a lesson that day that all men are not the same and it did not pay to accuse others in the wrong.

Life continued in school until the Primary Cert. We worked harder, did more homework and had some late evenings in school. Also, there was a lot of praying. Two or three Rosaries said each day and there were prayers to send supervisors who were supposed to be good at helping out with exams and that sort of thing. The day came at last. I think it was always on a Friday. Mrs Rowley, the teacher in a local school, was in charge that day. She seemed to be a very nice woman.

When that day was over we had some time left in school until the holidays, but with little to do. Priests, brothers, and nuns came trying to recruit us for the foreign missions. I think we all filled in forms agreeing to join but none of us wanted to. Martin J wanted me to be a priest but I didn't like the idea at all.

Culmore School Band c1955

Chapter 9

SECONDARY SCHOOL

I liked school but I never thought of what I should do when I left school. Farming seemed to be the most likely thing to do. At that time, where there were big families of up to ten or eleven, almost all the kids went to England or America and one would stay at home and look after the land and in some cases at that time they all left and the parents lived on their own into old age. In my case, I was the only child and was expected to take over the place anyway. Not many kids went to secondary school. Town kids did so because there could be a chance of getting a job as a guard or a civil servant or whatever state job was available.

Some country kids went for secondary education but there would have been money in the family. Parents would have been in America or a father would have worked hard in England and the mother would have been a saver and wanted to have a priest in the family. In most family homes there was very little interest in education. Work on the land was hard and the harder you could work the better you could survive. However, one could see in school the kids whose parents were interested in education were that little bit brighter and would always have the home lessons done. Most of us would dodge home lessons and try to do them the next day in school if we could get the time. Vocational schools were beginning to start up at that time and they were very good for young lads who went to England and were working in the building trade. They could start as carpenters' helpers and block layers' helpers and helpers in all the other trades and after a while they would know the job inside out. The time spent in the vocational school gave them confidence.

Martin James urged me to go to the College in Swinford and I did. It was nearly all priests who taught there. Jack O'Neill was the boss. He was from Killala. He taught botany and I think some Irish. He could get carried away about flowers and gardens and anything that grew. He was a pleasant man and his class passed quickly. Sean Leonard was known as Leonard. I think he was from Tubbercurry. He taught Maths and was very witty. Sometimes he would ask a question of a pupil at the end of the class, and if they couldn't answer it he would give whoever was near him a clip on the ear. He would use a swear word from time to time and he didn't sound like the usual priest. John McNicholas was from Swinford. He taught English and I enjoyed his classes very much. His stories about writers were new to me and he was very good on poetry. The poetry he did was more advanced than what we learned in the National School and he made it come alive in the class.

The next priest was Fr Towey from Ballaghadereen. He belonged to a footballing family and I think he was chairman of the Mayo GAA at one time. The last priest I remember was Liam Cawley. He was from somewhere in Sligo and had relations around Charlestown. Later he became parish priest of Charlestown. The last teacher was not a priest. Seamus Mangan was from Doohoma near Belmullet and was the Irish teacher. He was a very pleasant man who called every pupil Vickie which was the Irish for son. Because of that he was known as Vickie by all the pupils. He loved Irish and tried his best to get the language across but everything was against him.

There was no support for Irish in the homes and the state forced it on the pupils and did all the wrong things to make it attractive. The people who supported Irish in the town were a small group of teachers, a lawyer in Swinford, a guard from Connemara, and some others. They kept it a closed circle. They never involved working class people. Going to Saint Patrick's was OK in one sense. One learned new stuff and got to know other lads from places like Kiltimagh and Foxford. Also, I got to know more about the priests. Until then, the only time I saw a priest was at Mass or at school. Now I was living with them for most of the week. They were acting like average people and if they had a fault one could spot it very quickly. They were smokers and drinkers and would have arguments among themselves when they thought no one was looking.

I remember a retreat was held and it was on for about a week. A strange priest came. I think he was a Marist. He lectured a number of times each day and there were more break times. However, there was to be no talking during break which was not easy. That rule was broken pretty often by the younger lads. The fifth years tried to control that by warning them that they would be reported. When that didn't work, they would give a young fellow a clip across his ear. Some of them would use this opportunity to chastise someone they didn't like. After the retreat Canon Stenson's brother died and there was a mass which all the school had to attend. When that was over, the older lads asked Jack O'Neill for the day off and he agreed.

The next thing that happened was the death of Pope Pius XII. There were lectures about him. After that John XXIII was elected. The name John was a big surprise and Liam Cawley gave a lecture on that subject. I guess he had to do some research. The last John went back a very long way. The John before that was also John XXIII. It appears that at the time there were three popes all claiming to be the right pope. There was trouble between France and Italy. The French insisted the Pope live in France and a number of them did. However, it was decided to do something about the church breaking up so they got that John to call a consistory of the cardinals. The result of that was that a new pope was elected. He was Martin V. I had never known that there was ever a Pope Martin. That there were five of them was a big surprise. Cawley explained that the John who preceded Martin had been a trader or ship owner or businessman who had been ordained so that he could become pope. It was new to me that the church acted like that.

As school life continued the next thing that came up was paying for the year in school. It had never happened before and I knew my mother wouldn't like paying. Money was very scarce at that time and there were other expenses throughout the year. The money wasn't paid and nothing was said but I began to think about the future. Five years seemed a long time to spend there when one could be getting work done at home. At the end of the five years there might be nothing to show for it. I was interested in the land and always looked back to my father's time when something new would be happening and he had plans for the year ahead and the year after that. Country kids learned how to do hard work like their fathers and would emigrate like their fathers and grandfathers did before them.

The neighbours were working the land, they seemed to be getting on OK. I thought I could stay and work the land and raise cattle and I should manage OK. I gave up school and started working and planning what I should do for the next few years. There was one cow and a year-old heifer and a bull calf on the land at the time. I thought I would keep the heifer for a cow and let the bull calf go to a two-year-old. There was no loose money about to do anything else. I had been doing the farm work for the last five years at least, like saving a couple of acres of hay, sowing enough potatoes and vegetables and growing about a half-acre of oats. Paddy Molloy used to plough the land and cut the hay. It seemed to me that with a little help when necessary I could manage.

CHAPTER 10

POLITICAL AWARENESS

Over the years, once I had learned to read, I read as much as I could. Aunt Mary Kate used to bring me a lot of magazines but the trouble was they were religious magazines ranging from the Far East, The Messenger, Blessed Martin, to St Anthony and a lot more of that kind. However, my mother started buying the Irish Press on a Friday so I started getting a better picture of everyday life in Ireland and abroad. I used to hear people talking about politics and changing governments and at election time after mass on Sunday there would be men standing on a wall or a fence outside the church shouting and there would be a lot of the men on the ground shouting back at them. This only happened at election time and would go on for at least three Sundays. It was good fun.

After a while I began to cop on to what it was all about. I had a vague memory of the election of 1948. My father was alive then and I remember the postman, Jim McKenna, bringing a lot of little books and pictures. One picture of a man sticks out more than the others and I wonder now was it a picture of Sean McBride. I had heard of DeValera and I got the impression that my father hated him. However, after my father died, my mother always said he was a great man. At Bushfield Church the first election I remember was in 1950.

It was a council election and there was a big lorry parked outside the church and all of the men who were speaking were standing on it.

I discovered later that it belonged to John McIntyre, better known as John Con. His father was Con McIntyre who had been a councillor back in 1920. John Junior was now running for election. He ran a bottling plant in Charlestown and was a very wealthy man. After the election, I heard that he had lost by ten votes. However, another man from Clooncoose on the far side of Charlestown, Tommy Tarpey, was elected representing the Clann na Talmhan or The Farmers Party. The next election was in 1951, when the government changed and DeValera got back into power. I remember that before the election new ration books had been issued but when the new government got in they finished rationing which had been in force because of the war. Some shopkeepers were very worried that they would lose business because if your ration book was in a certain house you could not shop anywhere else. When the rationing was finished you could move to any shop you wanted to.

At Bushfield Church one Sunday, Douglas Kelly was standing on the fence speaking. A lot of people down on the road were shouting back at him. He had a very hard time trying to get through his speech. The following Sunday, Dominick Cafferky turned up. He was a TD at the time. He and Kelly were in The Farmers Party. He said, "Mr Kelly was asked questions last Sunday, I will answer them today". He gave a long speech but there was only silence from the ground. Not one question was asked. Kelly was a well-educated trained solicitor. As far as I know, Cafferky had very little formal education, but when it came to the cut and thrust of politics, Cafferky was unbeatable. If anyone asked a nasty question that day his answer would make them a laughingstock. He served two terms as TD and was chairman of Mayo County Council for five years. But after that he lost elections. The last time I saw him was many years later at a meeting in Kilkelly when there was an attempt to set up a Mart. He wanted to have one in Kilkelly. Other towns were pressing their case as well, but Cafferky was putting a strong case for Kilkelly. Another meeting was arranged for Kilkelly and Tom Peyton and myself went to it. When we got there the first news we heard was that Dominick Cafferky had died from a heart attack that evening. That was the end of the Mart in Kilkelly.

The next election was in 1954. Martin James Cassidy had run in the 1951 Dail Eireann election but wasn't running in 1954. I was in Culmore school at the time and Cafferky called in one day. They may have been arranging a meeting. On the day of the count, Sean Flanagan came in and Martin James introduced him to the class. Flanagan had been a TD from 1951. He was also captain of the Mayo football team which won the All-Ireland finals of 1950 and 1951. Another great player who played with Flanagan was Padraig Carney who was taught in our school, Culmore. His mother taught there. He became a doctor and was flown home a couple of times to help Mayo win matches. Culmore had another player on the Mayo team shortly after Carney. He was Jimmy McDonagh who was also a very good player. Flanagan's visit to the school was an exciting interlude and broke up our day. He was elected that day and spent his life in politics after that.

In that year or perhaps 1955 there was an election in England. Churchill who was the leader in the war had retired and Anthony Eden took over as leader of the Conservative Party and was elected. I was surprised when I discovered that the British election extended to part of Ireland also. It was the first time I discovered that six northern counties were part of Britain. As time went on, I read everything about what was going on in the North. I found that two MPs were elected representing the Sinn Fein party, which I had never heard of before. It was a republican party and my mother used to praise the Fianna Fail because they were republican. As the weeks went on, I read of a court case in the north where Philip Clarke who was elected MP for Fermanagh-South Tyrone was removed as MP and the man who lost the election Lord something or other was put in place. A week after, there was another court case held in which Tom Mitchell who was MP for Mid Ulster was disqualified and a new election was called.

The by-election was held and Tom Mitchell ran again for Sinn Fein and was elected with a bigger majority. In the following weeks there was another court case at which time Mitchell was disqualified and the Unionist called Beattie who lost the election was declared the new MP. This seemed very unfair to me and there was no way of doing anything about it. After reading more about the situation in the North, I discovered that the reason Mitchell, Clarke, Eamon Boyce, and the others were in jail was because they were involved in a barrack raid at which they were captured and they were sentenced to ten and twelve years in jail. There seemed to be no other way of beating the corrupt system.

Some months after he was declared MP, Beattie had to resign from the Westminster parliament because he held office of profit under the Crown so another by-election had to be called in Mid Ulster. Tom Mitchell ran again for Sinn Fein. The Unionists this time ran a man called Forrest. He classed himself as an Independent. The Catholic powers that be in the North which consisted of the bishops, wealthy "Castle" Catholics and those who held jobs under the system came to Dublin for advice. They lived well off the system. They didn't want to change and Tom Mitchell was getting too popular for their liking and posed a threat to their good life. I guess those people today would be classed as SDLP. Looking back now after sixty-five years, the picture is much clearer than then, but even then a child's mind could see what was right and what was wrong. The system in the 26 Counties was run by three parties who were enemies in the Civil War. They were corrupt with each other and corrupt with the people. The Church ruled over the parties and was very corrupt living off the system north and south. They didn't want change.

The advice they gave the "Castle" Catholics from the North was to put up a candidate against Tom Mitchell. They picked some well off person and the election went on. When the count was over Forrest had won with about 28,000 votes but Tom Mitchell had got over 24,000 votes. The Catholic candidate got about 5,000. The real victor was Mitchell. That was the first time I began to learn how the country was governed and how it was made up of two states: the North, a Protestant state, and the South, a Catholic state.

This election in the North made a big impression on me and stayed with me all my life. I don't remember much about 1956 in relation to other happenings but on the 12th of December 1956 the IRA launched a bombing campaign in the North against the British. It involved attacking barracks, army patrols and other things. It was a very active campaign for a period of time and on New Year's Day 1957 two IRA men, Sean South and Fergal O'Hanlon, were killed in an attack on a police barracks. There were very big funerals for these men, in particular for Sean South who was from Limerick. There were also songs written about them which are still sung down to the present day. That campaign went on until 1962 when a ceasefire was declared. It was not a success because it didn't involve those in the North and most of the people involved were from the South. To be successful it would have to have started in the streets of Belfast and Derry and be started by the youth.

In the South, the government fell in March 1957 and an election was held in May. This time Fianna Fail and DeValera were returned to power with their biggest majority ever. The times were bad then and the government had to borrow from Guinness to keep afloat. That was joked about for a long time after but the change didn't bring any improvement.

In the election Sinn Fein won four seats which they had never done since the 20s. The new TDs were: a relation of Fergal O'Hanlon in Monaghan, Rory O'Brady (Ruairi O'Bradaigh) in Longford, John Joe Rice in Kerry and John Joe McGirl in Sligo. They didn't take their seats in the Dail. This was a mistake but the policy was a hangover from events after the treaty. It wasn't a good tactic then and in 1957 it was a worse tactic. They hadn't learned from the past. In 1959 there was a presidential election and also a referendum to change the way of voting from the transferable vote to a single vote system.

Fianna Fail felt if they could change the method of voting they would have a better chance of getting elected in future elections. They also nominated DeValera for president.

DeValera won the presidential election with a big majority but Fianna Fáil lost the referendum so there was no change in the voting system. However, they remained a strong party for years after and got clear majorities in government. Lemass was put to the people as a leader who was very different to DeValera. He was on the political forefront for over forty years and in all that time things had got no better. In fact, they had got worse. The population had been dropping slowly but surely. There was no new industry to create jobs. Small farming was the only industry in the west and that wouldn't have survived if the farmer hadn't gone to England for a good part of the year to earn money so that his wife and kids could live in some comfort. It was they who kept the towns going along with other emigrants from England and America who came home from time to time and kept a sort of tourist industry going and sent money like there was no tomorrow.

Lemass was put forward as the leader who would change all that. A five-year plan was proposed and they sought membership of the EU or the EEC as it was called then. The country also became a member of the United Nations. Fianna Fail had a good propaganda machine at that time and they had a good newspaper owned by the DeValera family. The Sunday Press was the best-selling paper in Ireland at the time. There would be stories on the one hand about the War of Independence and Civil War.

Some of the party members like Sean McGlynn and Dan Breen had been heroes in that war and they always reminded the leaders of that fact. On the other hand, there were stories about the new five-year plan which would bring about a change in the economy and if a new company came there from the US which was happening at Shannon airport at the time, that would be boosted up. Things were a little bit better than in the middle 50s when there was a recession. The price of cattle was better but there is an up and down time for cattle prices and for any other kind of livestock or goods produced on a farm. Perhaps there was good weather at the time but things did seem to be better than in the years after the war.

Chapter 11

FARMING

The government had given a couple of new types of grants. One was if you kept an extra heifer for a cow you would get a grant. It may have been £20 at the time. I held on to two heifers at the time as my land was very under stocked. I also applied for a grant to reclaim a field which my father had started working on a couple of years before he died. Bushes and whins and brooms were growing up wild on the land and the brooms in particular seem to thrive on the red sandy soil. There were ridges where my father had some potatoes and turnips and didn't live to do them out.

The agriculture inspector came out to put a plan together. His name was Paddy McGirl. I didn't know for a long time afterwards that he was a brother of John Joe McGirl who had been elected Sinn Fein TD for Sligo-Leitrim. He may well have been in jail at the time because he had been sentenced to ten years by a military court. He checked out the land. A lot of levelling would have to be done, some fences knocked and the land would have to be rotovated. Ploughing would not work. Only a rotovator could level the ridges.

He said the grant would be small. He hinted maybe £20. That wasn't much good. However, when I got the plan back it was £56. At the time money was very scarce and doing the field could cost way beyond that.

Apart from the rotovating there would have to be seed and fertiliser bought, and the seeding done and the ground then harrowed and rolled. The year before, there was a scheme in which you could lime and fertilise the land and have the cost put on the rent over a period of years. My neighbour Tom Peyton was telling me about it and said he was going to apply for it so we both did the scheme. I had been wondering if it would be possible to get a loan from the bank. I didn't think it likely because I remembered a very honest man being in the bank one day who wanted to change a cheque and the bank man said he couldn't change it because he didn't know him. He told the man he should go to a shopkeeper he knew and perhaps he would change it for him. However, I decided to ask anyway. I went in one day and talked to the manager. His name was Morrissey-Murphy, a double-barrelled name.

His attitude was as I had expected. However, he said if I could get someone to sign for me he would agree to it. I mentioned it to Tom Peyton. He said he had also applied for a loan. I guess it would have been a big loan because he was going building sheds and other improvements. In his case, his father Harry had had two or three well paid jobs in his time and would have been well off. That didn't mean he would take any chances with loans and would never have borrowed money himself. However, some days later Tom told me he had seen the manager and I should call to him. I did so and after a lot of lecturing and advice I got my £100. I got my reclamation done. Tom Mulligan, a lad my own age had purchased a rotovator, the first about the place at the time. He did the job and Paddy Molloy did the harrowing and seeding and I had an extra field about three acres in size.

I had started drawing the dole at the time, about £18 a week, which was a help if you were not drinking or smoking which I was not at that time. In the summer it would be stopped and start back again in November. There were some extra cattle on the place and there was a bullock over two years old which I decided to sell. After school I started going to the pictures with my school friends: Martin and Francie Fenlon, Chris Brett, Frank Peyton and others. We used to meet up with another lad, Jimmy Weever, who was some years older and had been in England. He used to deal a little in cattle and would help other farmers at fairs. I asked him to give me a hand with the bullock and he said he would. We took the bullock to the fair in Swinford. I am not sure what time of the year it was. It may have been in spring. The fair was always on Wednesday. We set off in the early morning at about seven or eight o'clock. He was a quiet animal. I don't think we had a halter on him. As we got near the town there would be dealers asking the price and offering different prices. Most people would not sell on the road but would spend some time at the fair first.

We got a number of bids of over £60 at the fair and in the end we accepted a bid of £65. The buyer was Tom Noone from Tubbercurry. He had bought a lorry of cattle that day and he was a big buyer at the time.

The following month we were at the Charlestown fair and after looking at all the cattle for sale, we bought a yearling strawberry heifer for something like twenty-four or twenty-five pounds. We bought her off Tom Duffy from Kilkelly who dealt in those kinds of cattle. That heifer became a great cow and was in my herd for many years after. Jimmy Weever was a great help to me for many years until the fairs were replaced by the marts. My herd increased over the next ten years to thirteen or fourteen cows.

Chapter 12

FCA Days

At the time some of my friends had joined the FCA. Martin and Francie Fenlon and Eamon Gallagher were joining it so I joined in November 1959. On a Monday night in the backroom of the town hall in Swinford myself and Chris Brett from Corthoon and Liam Rooney from Swinford were signed on by Captain Art Hume. He was a native of County Meath. He was a very intelligent man and was one of the finest people I ever met. Chris has been in England all his life and some years afterwards Liam Rooney became a Christian Brother and later became a priest. I think he is now in Scotland.

The FCA was good fun. We got a uniform and a 303 rifle. We would have a meeting every Monday night and most Saturdays there would be a Field Day when we would be picked up by an army truck and taken to a shooting range or on tactics or manoeuvres. Frank Callinan was the regular Quartermaster Sergeant who was responsible for uniforms and weapons and all stuff used for training. Corporal Pat Hynes did all the training, marching, foot drill, arms drill, anything that involved using the guns and oiling and cleaning them, loading and unloading them. He also trained us in dealing with hand grenades which could be very dangerous if one found a live one and didn't know what it was.

I remember being told the story many times of a neighbour of mine who was working in a hardware store in Charlestown. He found a hand grenade in the store one day, a round iron object of about a pound and a half in weight. He didn't know what it was and pulled out a pin which released the lever causing the striker to ignite the fuse). He was killed on the spot.

At first there was only one gun being used but the following year a lot of other guns were introduced. There was the Bren which had a magazine holding 30 rounds and was in use all over the world. Then there was the Gustav which was a short light gun and was used in street fighting. Then there was the Vickers machine gun. This was a gun that would be mounted in a particular spot as support for the infantry. There was a team of five men to manage the Vickers. It had to be mounted on a tripod. No. 1 was in charge of that and he also fired the gun. No. 2 fitted the gun on the tripod and lay beside it. Nos.3, 4 and 5 supplied the ammunition and water. Water was required because the Vickers could use five hundred rounds per minute. In that case the barrel would get red hot so it had to be cooled. The barrel was encased in a wider barrel which was scaled with a pipe leading into a can of about five gallons of water. The water kept circulating and kept the barrel cool. The gun was fed ammunition by a belt containing two hundred and fifty rounds. The belt had to be filled carefully and evenly. It was fed into the gun by the No. 2 who had to keep it steady while the gun was being fired. The gun was used first in the WWI, not so much in the Second World War but it was brought into use again in the Korean War where the Chinese used to send a human wave of soldiers over a mountain and the Vickers would have the speed to cut them down. The trouble with the Vickers was that there could be a lot of stoppages. This also made it very interesting. There are four position stoppages. The crank handle would stop in a certain position and you knew what was wrong when it stopped.

The first almost always involved just reloading. The second was almost always involving the belt feeding the gun. A round may not have been put in level with the other rounds or the belt would be moving up and down very fast when the gun was firing and would cause cross loading. Sometimes you could get a telescopic round with the gun failing to eject the empty shell and the following rounds entering into the empty shell would cause a problem. There were tools supplied to solve that problem. The other faults I can't remember now. There were four phases of each position fault which could happen but seldom did. The Swinford section was in charge of the Vickers. The Charlestown section was in charge of the mortar section. The Mortar was a gun that was very much in use all over the world at that time. We had two sizes of mortar. The larger one would fire a large bomb a longer distance. It consisted of a heavy metal base plate which was laid on level, solid ground. The gun itself looked like a length of pipe about two yards long with a fitting at the closed end of the barrel which locked into the baseplate. The third section consisted of two legs attached to a fitting which circled the barrel. The sights were fitted on to this and it could be also manipulated up or down and left and right. The bomb was dropped into the barrel and hit a striker down at the base plate. The bomb shot into the air at once. A member of the team would be watching with binoculars some distance forward to see if it landed in the right place.

The first shot might not be accurate because the baseplate would not be settled into the ground. After the first shot it would not move much more. The small mortar was much lighter and could be carried about much more easily. The Viet Cong used it to great effect in Vietnam. It was one of the reasons why they won the war. We could shoot the Vickers on the local ranges but Charlestown had to go to the Glen of Imaal to fire the mortar. Field Days were enjoyable and passed Sundays quickly and sometimes there would be a weekend camp for shooting on the Galway or Finner ranges. However, the summer yearly camp was the best time of the year.

Finner Camp between Bundoran and Ballyshannon was where most of the West of Ireland members went to. Swinford was 'C' Company, Westport, Ballina, Claremorris and Enniscrone also had companies. Castlebar and Sligo were different types of companies. One was Transport and the other Signals. There were other names, official names for them but I forget them now. All the companies in Mayo were known as the 18th battalion. Roscommon was the 19th Battalion. We were infantry which just meant men with guns and were always deployed on the ground. Castlebar and Sligo were support companies which did transport and signals and there were other companies in bigger towns which did artillery and tanks and stuff like that.

It was a long journey to Finner in an army lorry. About thirty of us travelled there on a fine sunny day. The sides of the lorry had a cloth type of covering and could be rolled up. This was the case on that day so we had a great view of the countryside. I noted as we went through Sligo that in places the fields were bigger and also the hay cocks were much bigger than the ones we made at home and they seemed to be left in the field for a long time as the aftergrass was growing high again. At home our hay would be left in cocks in the field for a week or two and then made into a pike or a reek. I noted other things which I cannot remember now that were different on farms. I also caught a glimpse of the sea a few times and at Bundoran town. Finner was a couple of miles further and in open country. It was near the sea. There was a lot of land fenced off and sandhills near the sea. Some of the sandhills had whatever kind of grass cover taken off them and the wind was blowing the fine sand high into the air. We got into the camp and unloaded from the lorry. There were some large buildings, all made of wood. I discovered later they were the cookhouses and stores. There were lines of smaller buildings each the size of a house also made of wood. There was a number on each door. We were told to go to a particular number because that was where we had to sleep. We had a look inside and found there was a line of beds laid out along each wall.

The beds consisted of three wide boards laid on two trestles about six inches high at each end of the boards. On top of the boards was a mattress together with a number of blankets folded with two sheets. We had to choose a bed first and then dress it. I remember Martin Fenlon and Chris Brett were next to me. I knew some of the other lads but some of them I had never met before. After that we were rounded up and marched to the cookhouse by, I think, Sergeant John Cleary from Ballyhaunis. The tables were laid out the same as the beds, lined along each wall, six men to a table. The food came out on plates. It was in one lump in the centre of the plate. It had a green colour but we couldn't figure out what it was. The green stuff seemed to be beans and they were mashed up with potatoes and there may have been something else. However, we were very hungry and had to eat it. Some of the lads who had been there before said it would settle down as the week went on.

After that we inspected the place, had a look at a fine football pitch, things which looked like ball alleys but were in fact short shooting ranges and in the camp itself we saw square areas of concrete which looked like swimming pools but due to the fact that everything was built of wood they were making sure there was plenty of water about in case of a fire. There was also a canteen where one could get minerals, mostly orange, and buns and sweet cake. There was also Guinness, beer and whiskey served there but we were young at the time and didn't have much money anyway. We all went to bed about eleven or twelve. I slept well which surprised me as it was my first time sleeping anywhere other than at home but it was very comfortable.

In the morning we were woken very early by a camp orderly who would have been up all night. He had some type of baton with him which he banged on the door and the timber walls while shouting loudly at the same time. The fact that he had been awake all night, probably against his will, gave him great pleasure in rousing others out of a very comfortable sleep. Having dressed, the next thing to do was to get washed. There was a large new building which had toilets, washrooms and shower rooms.

It was the only concrete building in the camp. It was on the outer edge of the camp close to the road to Ballyshannon. After that we were rounded up by a Sergeant and marched to the cook house. The food in the morning was much nicer than the evening before and more like a normal breakfast. I think we wandered back to our huts and sat around for a while. Then there was more shouting with orders being given and each company was marched on to the square. It was a grid of land over an acre in size. Each company sent one marker to the square and they took up positions so many yards apart at the far end. Each company marched toward its own marker. Then they were joined by the officers. Eddie Boland was captain of Swinford C Company and Paddy Gordon and Mickie McNeela were lieutenants.

At that time Douglas Kelly was commandant which was the highest position in the FCA but he didn't go to camp and retired some time afterwards. We remained at ease for some time. Then a regular officer appeared. He was a colonel and was in charge of the camp for the fortnight. We were brought to attention, then stood at ease again and he gave a talk on what we had to do and how we should behave and if we didn't behave there would be dire consequences. After he finished the sergeant major took over. He was a Donegal man called Gallagher. He had a strong voice which suited his job as sergeant major and he was very much in charge. However, at the end of it all he was a very pleasant man and if anyone was in trouble he would see to it that it was sorted out. He lectured on the everyday running of the camp. He referred to the issue of the pass which we were all given, going to town and getting back at a particular time, the use of lights, toilets and showers. He warned against drinking too much. He also gave a strong warning about the sea. The River Erne entered the sea very near the camp. At the point of entry there were whirlpools which were very dangerous.

He also referred to Tullaghan Strand which had in the past and down to the present day claimed the lives of many swimmers. Monday morning was the start of a very busy week. We were woken up early each morning by an orderly sergeant. Each company marched to breakfast. After, the buttons and shoes had to be shone and polished and then each company marched on to the square to their particular markers. Their officers fell in and at the front of the soldiers there were three officers standing on their own. The colonel was the boss in the camp, then there was a commandant, and a third man was a captain. The captain would come to attention, turn to the commandant, salute him and shout something at him. Then the commandant would turn to the colonel, salute and shout something. Next the colonel would turn to the assembled ranks and shout, "Carry on with the programme".

There the companies would break into sections of ten or twelve men. A corporal would take over. The sections would be marched away to different places where training would take place. For a start, it was arms drill but as time went on the stripping and dissembling of the rifle and the Bren gun and the Gustav were dealt with. Also we got training in the use of hand grenades.

On that first day we were issued with rifles in the store and we had to sign for them. For the rest of the camp we had to keep them with us, remember the number and of course clean them. That was no easy task because they could be inspected after each class and the big problem in Finner in the dry weather was the blowing sand. It got everywhere, even into the huts where we were sleeping. Sometimes you could see sand on the white sheets and if you were drinking a bottle of orange, if it was left for a time you would find sand on the neck of the bottle. We would have our last meal of the day at about 5:30 pm and by 10 o'clock we would be hungry again so we would have to go to the canteen and get orange and a pastry so that we didn't feel hungry going to bed. I think they were supposed to give out tea and a slice or two of bread in the cook house later in the evening but no one in the camp knew about it and the workers in the cookhouse might not have wanted the trouble of it. Late in the second week when money was spent up they started making up a barrel of soup which was given out late in the evening.

Many of the young lads got their cupful and some went back for a second and third fill. Not being used to it, some of them were very sick the next morning. Late in the second week we fired the rifle on a huge shooting range near to sea. It was six yards for shooting purposes, but the area was much bigger, perhaps hundreds of acres. There were sheep grazing all over the place and when they wandered into the shooting area we were told to stop firing and a number of lads would chase them off and we would continue. However, on range day, the practice could go on for a long time and about half the men would miss their dinner and they would get dinner and supper combined but it still was only one meal. One other big project in the early days of the camp was the medical inspection.

The sergeant major gave an order to a company sergeant to round up the men, about six hundred of them, and find a quiet secluded place where the inspection could be carried out. We were directed to a spot behind the large new toilet and washroom building where we could be seen from the camp, which didn't matter as almost everyone in the camp was being inspected. An officer carrying a cane under his arm came on the scene. He may have been a doctor, and after giving the order to strip off everything, he and the sergeant started inspecting. The sergeant had a notebook and would take notes if he saw anything unusual. One thing the sergeant hadn't noticed was that we were very near the road. It was a tourist area and there were a lot of buses passing and we could see the passengers standing up and staring at 600 naked people.

We got paid on Thursday. The army pay was about £3.10 per week. We had got paid the week before but along with our £3.10 we also got a `gratuity` of £6 which was very good money at that time, 1960. That night, there was a party in the canteen for the 18th Mayo

Battalion. There were mostly the younger lads who were drinking minerals but the older men, officers of the FCA and regular army men, were drinking Guinness and whiskey.

I remember at that time, 1960, that a glass of Guinness was eight old pence. You got four pence back out of a shilling. It was cheaper in the army camps and barracks than in the pubs. The party went on a long time and a lot of people sang and gave recitations and performed in other ways. I remember Dessie McIntyre from Charlestown sang "Noreen Bawn". He was a good actor also and had parts in many of the plays that Charlestown Dramatic Society produced. Commandant Peadar Kilroy from Newport sang "The Queen of Connemara", a song about a boat. He was a very good singer. The next morning, Friday, we had our breakfast, we gathered up our stuff, got into the army lorry again and started for home. The sides of the lorry were rolled up, it was a lovely summer's day and we enjoyed our trip home.

That winter, in November, some of us did a camp in Renmore Barracks in Galway. This time we were doing a training course on the Vickers machine gun. We spent the whole fortnight learning about that gun. This time we didn't get a gratuity so it was just two weeks army pay. Galway was a different place to Finner and it was wintertime. It was all stone buildings built around a square. There were two storey buildings, they were known as blocks. There was an entrance in the centre of each block and there were two billets left and right. They were numbered as A Block, B Block, C Block. We were billeted in A Block on the left on the ground floor. There was a fireplace on the gable wall and as far as I knew, that was the only heat there was in the place but we were young and had plenty of blankets and were active and didn't feel the cold. I guess there were about twenty men in billets and they were from Swinford and Westport. The Swinford men I remember were Eugene Harrington, Dessie McIntyre, Tom McGowan, Eddie Joe Haran, T. McNulty, Muldowney and Tom O'Hara. The lads I most remember from Westport were Padraig McGreal and Jackie Foley.

Padraig's brother Jack was a captain at the time and he had another brother Michael who was a priest. Fr Michael became very well known in later years as a great supporter of the Irish language, the opening up of the railways in the west and also as a writer. Jackie Foley was working for the [Mayo] Vocational Education [Committee] and responsible for the FAS schemes all over the County.

The Vickers course was a great success. Corporal Kerr was a young regular soldier. He taught us over the fortnight. He was a good teacher, quietly in control and at the end of the course we knew almost everything that was to be known about the Vickers. We went to Galway some nights to films and other times to walk about the town.

There was a narrow walkway from Renmore into the bus station and The Great Southern Hotel and onto Eyre Square. I remember the statue of Padraic O'Conaire in a seated position, wearing a hat, looking onto the park. Having seen what could be seen, we didn't drink and couldn't afford to, we headed back the quiet, dark walkway to the barrack.

Many years later, I heard on the news one morning of a young foreign student who been murdered on that walkway. It was dark and not a place to be alone at night. In the billet at night there was always great fun. There was no TV at that time and if a shirt had to be washed we had to do it ourselves. I remember one guy washing a shirt and trying to dry it at the fire. There was a lot of fun and craic going on, so he turned his back to the fire, holding the shirt behind him and joined in the fun. A minute later his shirt had disappeared. There was a great draw in those chimneys which were made a hundred years before and his shirt had been drawn up the chimney. They were a fine group of lads there that winter of 1960. Swinford and Westport always got on well and seemed to have a lot in common. That was the year the 32nd battalion went to the Congo and a section of about eight of them were killed. It was debated about a lot in the barracks. I guess at that time we didn't know the full story of what was going on in the Congo.

In fact, we didn't know the story at all and the Irish troops were not prepared for the climate or the war situation at that time or in the years that followed. It brought home to us young lads who were learning about guns and military tactics, what war was like and there were regular soldiers in the barracks who knew some of the men who were killed. There was a mass said in the church in Galway one morning, attended by the Bishop, the mayor, city councillors and TDs and all the important people in the city. We all marched out from the barracks to attend it.

I think the name of the sergeant major at that time was Tom McHugh. We were told he was a very strict and important man but according to people I met after who served under him, he was a very pleasant and helpful man. The following year, I did another winter camp in Galway. I think it was an NCO course. On that course, Kevin Stenson from Culmore and Shea Cribbin from Kilkelly were with me. Gerry Tierney, a corporal in the regular army, was in charge. He was also an old schoolmate. The lieutenant in overall charge was a young fellow from Leitrim. I cannot remember his name now but he went on to become Chief of Staff of the Irish Army.

Shea Cribbin was a good singer and he went on to become the leader of the Riviera Showband which was very popular in the 60s and 70s. Shea made a number of records. The showbands fizzled out after a time and Shea died young many years ago. That was my last camp in Renmore, but for years after we used to go on overnight camps and shoot on the range the following day.

I always went to Finner in the summer, but I did a couple of winter camps in Custume Barracks, Athlone. The first one was a Vickers course again. I thought I had learned everything about the Vickers but there was some new stuff and we learned a lot about tactics. We learned where you would set up a gun. You had to set it up where you had a good view of the enemy. Also, you would have to mount it where it would be hard to observe it from the air.

As there were always two Vickers within a short distance of each other to help teamwork and supply, it would not be easy to find cover. Gerry Tierney, Tom O'Hara and myself were together from Swinford. We fired the Vickers one day on the range and it-went on for a very long time. Next morning, I was very deaf. Once, when I didn't pick up what Gerry had said, he complained that my ears were much bigger than his and I should be able to hear much better than he could. The first week we were out in the country doing tactics. However, at the weekend Gerry developed a bad cough. On Sunday morning in church he made so much noise it was hard to hear the chaplain and he was immediately put in hospital. Tom and myself visited him often for the few days he was there. He explained the working of the hospital. The nurses would be classed as officers and may have held the rank of captain. I'm not sure if there was a doctor there as there would not be many patients there at any time. I remember afterwards talking to my neighbour, Jack Duffy. He was a captain in the IRA and after the Treaty was a Captain in the Free State Army. He told me he was a patient in that military hospital in 1922-23 and he said he witnessed the execution, by firing squad, while looking through a window, of a number of anti-Treaty men. He said the squad's guns were loaded by other soldiers and only every second gun was loaded and when the squad took up position, the officer in charge made the squad swap guns with each other. Then the order to fire was given and the men fell to the ground. Next the officer went to each of the executed men and, using his revolver, shot each of them in the head.

After a couple of days, Gerry Tierney was released and we carried on. We used to have good fun in the NCOs mess where billiards and pool were played. We would have a couple of glasses of beer and got to know a lot of the old timers who were great characters, great storytellers and very witty.

Some nights, we went into the town, Athlone. One half of the town was on the Connaught side of the Shannon and the other half was on the Leinster side. The Connaught side seemed to have the day-to-day services like butcher shops, barber shops, hardware shops and places that provided everyday services. There was a castle near the river. The pub nearest the castle had a key which was about one foot long and very big. They claimed it was the key of the castle. There were two cinemas and a lot of stylish fashion shops. The factories were there also. There was a woollen mill and factory which seemed to employ a lot of people, called Gentex. There was another smaller one called Sportex. There were four factories altogether and in the evenings the town was crowded with people going home from work mostly on bicycles at that time.

There seemed to be plenty of work in Athlone, and the army barracks added to the town also. On a side street, the former home of John Count McCormack was pointed out to us one night. He was the most famous Irishman of his time in the 1920s, 30s and 40s. We finished the camp in a very good mood. It was very enjoyable and we had learned a lot about Athlone and its history and the history of the army and the barracks itself. There was a block called "the new block" where we stayed which had a very big basement. It was rumoured that it would become the headquarters of the government if Ireland was hit by a nuclear bomb. At the time, there had to be some place in the event of a hit and I suppose that was as good a place as any other. There was an old block in the barracks called "Long Valley". If there was any trouble caused in the other blocks, the men would be warned that if it happened again, they would be sent to Long Valley. In fact, there was some trouble in our block one night and in the morning the sergeant major came around and warned everyone they would be sent to Long Valley if it happened again. He gave a stiff lecture as well even though he knew we had nothing to do with it. However, that is the way that the job was done and it could be very entertaining. Those men, corporals and sergeants and other non-commissioned officers didn't have much higher education but time and place had educated them. They had served in the army for years. When a newly commissioned officer straight out of college was put in charge, he would have to depend on them to show him the ropes. Sometimes a young officer would take over and start throwing his weight around. It would not be long until the place was up in a heap. The older senior officers would have a good laugh with the young fellow's discomfiture. The NCOs were very good teachers and every class was the best fun.

We heard many stories about Long Valley after. It was supposed to be haunted. However, there were men living there at the time and they didn't seem to have a problem. A couple of years ago, I was talking to a man from Athlone who said he had worked in Long Valley carrying out repairs and when he was working on a particular window, he was told that a man had hanged himself in that window. That may be where the story of the haunting came from. Gerry Tierney continued in the army for many years but died some years ago. Tom O'Hara went to England and I didn't see him for many years. He is retired now and comes home on holidays.

I did a second camp in Athlone some years after that. It was an NCOs course again but I was the only person from Mayo. The rest of my section came from Galway, Leitrim, Longford and one lad came from Offaly. We were doing field tactics and CSO Mickie Ahern was in charge. He was a widely known company sergeant and used to act as sergeant major in Finner during the summer. He had been to the Congo and told many stories of his time there. Many different countries had troops serving with the UN - Swedes, Indonesians, a number of African countries and Indians. Mickie reckoned that the Irish got on very well with the Indians. Both countries got their independence from Britain at the same time. Gandhi was a hunger striker as were many Irish patriots. The Irish army had a very small budget and couldn't afford to spend much money on arms and equipment while the Swedish army was from a very rich country and had been preparing for war from the 30s as they were afraid that Hitler would invade their neutral country. Therefore, in the Congo they were very much more advanced than the other neutral countries.

Another officer we had the pleasure of being involved with was Commandant Pat Quinlan. He had just returned from the Congo a couple of months before that. He would have been one of the leaders of the 35th Battalion. He and his men were sent into a province in the South of The Congo called Katanga run by a guy called Tshombe who had backed the Belgians before The Congo became a republic. When the Irish army moved in, they were attacked by Tshombe's men of whom there were thousands. I think the Irish had less than two hundred. The Irish dug well in and were supposed to have killed hundreds of the enemy.

The Irish had never lost a man. However, the Irish were running out of ammunition. They could get no support as far as military help was concerned so the UN must have managed to organise a ceasefire. They got out after some time but it was said later that they should not have been sent in in the first place. Over the years, there was an attempt made to blame Pat Quinlan for what happened but this is a great country for cover up, whether the mistake was made by the Irish army or the UN, I don't know. Conor Cruise O'Brien was in charge of the UN force for a time but he may have resigned by then. There was a film made a couple of years ago about the event and it could have gone some way towards clearing Pat Quinlan's name.

When he returned to Athlone, Commandant Quinlan was put in charge of civil defence and he delivered a number of lectures on the subject which involved protecting the environment and what to do in the event of a nuclear explosion. He concentrated on the nuclear fallout. It was very boring but he was a witty man and he kept a bit of fun going all the time. I remember one Monday morning after a weekend home, during which he got very little sleep, a lad called Connolly, I think, fell asleep in Quinlan's class. Quinlan gave him a good telling off but afterwards made a joke about it. I also remember when Sergeant Cecil Adams, who would be very much in charge, would get overpowering. One of the other sergeants who had been to Katanga with Quinlan would say, "I didn't see you around the tunnel Cecil." It seems a very serious battle had been fought around a particular tunnel and Cecil had never been to the Congo or Katanga so he would have to pipe down.

I think that would have been one of my last camps before going to England but many years later in the 80s I did two other camps in Castlebar Military Barracks. However, they were only for a week at a time and one could go home at times and pay was way ahead of the 60s.

Taken in Finner Camp, Donegal 1960/61

Taken in Renmore Barracks, Galway with Kevin Stenson 1961/62

Chapter 13

ENGLAND

By now, the farm was improving but at the same time one could see that the income was small and one could not make enough money to expand as a faster pace. There was no work worth talking about locally. All my generation used to go to England but they would stay there except for coming back for a holiday once a year. I didn't think I could do that because my mother and my aunt were at home. My mother could manage on her own for a short period, but I would need to be here most of the time to keep the show on the road. Also, I had a strong attachment to the land. It was a love hate relationship. But I remember from my first years of childhood, my father had a dream of developing the farm to its full potential. I felt that way too. A lot of the men who had stayed farming went potato picking in England from September to December and they used to make good money.

The sugar factories in England used to require a lot of labour also and I remember my next-door neighbour used to go there in the winter. People used to sign up for the campaign in the summer. The agent for the factories would call to the dole office on a particular day and take the names of the men who wanted to go. There were eighteen sugar factories in England at the time so a lot of men were needed, and they seldom turned down anyone.

However, there was one requirement: you had to be a certain age. I am not sure what it was. It may have been twenty-one. I had been warned about it because I may have been under the age at the time. I was interviewed by the agent, got my age right and was accepted. I would be informed later when and where I was going. In September, I got a letter with a free pass and telling me I was going to a place called Allscott near Wellington, Shropshire, England. The last couple of weeks at home were very busy. The cows were more or less dry or would be in the coming weeks. The potatoes had to be dug, there used to be quite a lot at that time, so I got Jimmy Weever to do that job and look after the cows when necessary.

A couple of days before they were leaving, some other lads who were going to different factories had their passes cancelled but mine held good. I think it was the 4th of October 1966, I got Mary Costello`s taxi to Swinford. There, I discovered that Padraic Durcan from Corthoon, with whom I had gone to school, was also going to Allscott. When we got on the bus for Claremorris, I found that there were others from Swinford. Michael and Willie Groarke from Cloontubrid had been going for years and Paddy Groarke from Meelick was going for the first time. There were also a number of lads from Ballina whom I got to know later. We got the train from Claremorris to Dublin and one thing I noticed when we were arriving in Dublin was the strong smell of coal. I guess turf had a smell also but I hadn't noticed it except in some houses where turf that contains sulphur was burned. That had a strong smell. We must have got a bus from the train to the Iveagh Hostel where we would stay the night and be sorted out the next day before going on the boat for England. We were fed in the Iveagh Hostel and given a number for a bed. Padraic Durcan and myself stayed together. I am not sure if we had a drink in a local pub or not, but we went to our numbered cubicles, one person per cubicle, to bed. There must have been hundreds of people staying in the hostel. That night as we talked before bed, we watched the porters who were very busy. They were shouldering people to their beds and I saw one of the men who was on the bus with us earlier being carried to bed.

In the morning, when we woke up, we saw lines of men carrying bowls and we figured they were used for toilet purposes and were being emptied. At breakfast, we got good food. It was a fry, with rashers, sausages and a fried egg. At home, I was used to boiled eggs and some porridge. I noticed a lot of the regular people who were there, in particular at dinner time, would buy their own food and that would not be much. I saw some of them buying a single potato and having some water with it.

Some of the people who were there may have been ex-army and could have been in the British or Irish army because from time to time they would salute someone just passing along or they would stand to attention or bark out orders or march quickly through the room for five or six yards. Some had physical problems, like being lame or having a limb missing, but most of them had mind problems or drink problems or were very depressed.

At home, one would see one or two people like that on a fair day but here in the Iveagh Hostel there seemed to be hundreds of them. It appeared they were very independent; some were very educated but had problems with life. I'm sure they could be cared for in homes but they wanted to be free and do their own thing. After breakfast, Padraic and myself decided to take a walk a bit further afield from the Iveagh and I suggested we get lost. We had no problem getting lost. Padraic said in that situation always ask a policeman. We did that but we had to ask three in all before we got back to the Iveagh. After a meal we were called into a room by the agent and were given our passes and some other paperwork and then a bus arrived to take us to the boat. Two or three of the residents decided they were going to the factory as well and came with us on the bus. They were younger and witty. They had nothing to do and might get a lift back on another bus again and if they didn't, they had all the time in the world to walk back.

It was the first time I was on a boat except for a small rowing boat. There was a huge number of people boarding. We were told by people who had travelled over and back before that it was also a cattle boat and there were cattle already on board. There was also a first- and second-class end. I think it was stated on our pass that we were second-class. We found places to leave our cases and wandered about looking at everything. We looked at the harbour and counted a huge number of other boats there, some of them larger than ours. There was a higher and lower deck so Padraic and I went down to the lower deck and discovered there was a bar there and there was a large number of men and a few women drinking. They would have been all seasoned travellers.

Some people on the boat even had dogs with them. We were told by a Dublin man that Dublin people often went shopping to Liverpool and I guess it happened the other way around as well. Eventually, the boat began to move. It twisted and turned for a bit, would stop suddenly and then move off again. Those of us who were standing had to hold onto something tightly or we would fall. After a few minutes the boat started up and continued on a straight course. After that, quite a few people started getting sick. Children, of whom there were a lot on board, were sure to get sick but older people didn't expect to and were taken by surprise. It was fine if one was leaning over the rails and it dropped into the sea, but soon the deck was covered with vomit and we had to be careful where we stepped. Also, it wasn't safe to stand facing people or you could become a victim. After a while, Padraic said he wasn't feeling well but his mother and father had thought of everything and had sent anti-sickness tablets with him. He took them and was OK. After that, I felt my stomach getting disturbed so I lay down on a pile of cases that had been stacked in a corner. After a while my stomach seemed to settle and we were able to start walking about again. We went down to the lower deck again and the bar was still crowded with men drinking faster and shouting louder than they were the first time we saw them.

After a while, we must have wandered into the first-class area. It seemed more stylish and was much quieter. Some people were sitting around talking quietly, like visiting a house at home. After a few minutes, a porter or sailor or whatever he was, told us to get out, so we did. We had a look over the rails and as the boat cut through the water it left a frothy wake behind it. As the night wore on, the bar must have closed and most of the men who had been there found a sheltered spot on the deck near the front of the boat and continued to talk or just sit around. After a long time, the boat slowed down and started jerking about and it was said it was pulling into port. However, it wasn't the end of our sea journey. We were in Birkenhead. We still had to go to Liverpool. The cattle were unloaded at Birkenhead. We watched them being unloaded and men with sticks driving them up the narrow lane. They didn't seem to be fat cattle, so perhaps they would graze some more in England before they were slaughtered. The boat moved on again, and after some time, pulled into Liverpool. It was daylight by now. There must have been someone representing the agent in charge of us, because two men were picked out of our group to be checked by the customs. Following that, we must have had food and then we were loaded on a bus for Allscott. At that time of the morning, there didn't seem to be many people in the streets. The buildings were all of red brick, in some cases blackened by soot I suppose and very high, with many storeys. After a short bit, we entered a tunnel and afterwards I was told it must have been the Mersey Tunnel. It was well lit and painted and where it was joined by another tunnel that area was tiled and I was surprised to see women with mops and buckets mopping and polishing the tiles. We continued in the tunnel for quite some time before emerging into open countryside.

It was a warm autumn day. The fields were very large with huge numbers of cattle in them. We were going so fast we didn't have time to count them, but there must have been over a hundred in some fields. When I thought of our Mayo countryside, five or six cattle would be the average number that would be in some of our fields. We passed through many built-up areas, but I cannot remember any towns until we came to Whitechurch which one of the lads who had been there before said was in Shropshire. However, we still had to travel a good while longer before we arrived at Allscott. The bus pulled into a parking area beside six round roofed buildings. They were a little like the army billets but were concrete and the base about four feet high, but the roof was rounded galvanise. Each hut was numbered and as there were three shifts in the factory, each shift got two huts. As there were about one hundred and twelve men over from Ireland, the place was almost full up. Someone told us we were on "C" shift so we took the "C" huts. We took our cases in and chose our beds and lockers.

After that, we were told to collect our blankets in another room. A tall good-looking woman was cleaning that end and was very friendly and joking and the men who had been there before knew her as well. We dressed our beds and were then brought to the canteen where we got food. I remember it was much nicer than the first food we got in Finner Camp years before. After that, we went to the huts again and unpacked and lay around for some time. Then someone mentioned the pub and most of us decided to go. It was only a short walk down the road. The name of it was "The Fox and Duck". I forget who the landlord was at the time. Padraic and myself had a pint of Mild each. It seemed to be a weaker drink than Guinness or the beer we used to drink at home.

The price of a pint was one shilling and ten pence which was cheaper than at home. There was no one drinking Guinness. After two drinks, we went back to the hostel. We talked to the night orderly whom I got to know later on and who became a very good friend of mine over all my years there. He was Con Keane from Athea in County

Limerick. We were starting work in the morning at 6 o`clock. He said he would call us, and he did. We were up at 5:30 and clocked in. My number, 180, was my number for all the years I was there.

It appears that a lot of work had been carried out on the factory over the summer and when they started it up the new works went wrong. We were put to work filling trenches and emptying areas that had flooded for several days. One day, we were finishing our shift at two. Willie Humbert from Ballina and myself were asked by a foreman to do a double shift, emptying an underground building which contained pumps and other stuff which we didn't know the use of. It was filling with water from the leaking pumps and we were supposed to empty it by taking the water out with buckets. We had to climb steep stairs to where there was a runoff at the top. We continued to do that for the eight hours of the shift except for our two tea breaks. We didn't see any foreman all day but near the end of the shift, a well-dressed man came down looking. The water started leaking faster. It hadn't got any higher or lower all day but the man told us to move faster. Willie Humbert who had been there before said the man was the manager of the factory, Roy Smith. As it was the end of our shift, almost ten o'clock, we left and clocked out. It was Sunday and I hadn't a clue about time and a half or double time. Willie knew all about it and said we would get double time. After another couple of days of that sort of work, the factory started up and wagons of beet started coming in again and that morning, we were taken into the factory.

There were three floors and there was a lift which serviced the three. I was taken up in the lift. I had never been in one before and was told how to use it. However, I used the stairs for some time after because I had seen some people get stuck in the lift and I didn't want to draw attention by that happening to me.

There were nine or ten square things, three or four yards long and two yards wide and four and a half feet high. There were also three much larger machines which looked like drums and were rotating all the time. We didn't have anything to do with them but the square ones on the floor were our job. They were called presses. There was one other tank like thing. It was a cloth washer and I was going to be in charge of that. There were two types of presses: thick juice presses and lime presses. The man in charge was Tom Bebbington. He was very heavy and didn't do any heavy work but kept walking around keeping an eye on things. He talked very fast with a local accent. I didn't know what he was saying but I guessed most of the time and always agreed with him. There were two Irish lads there who had been there for a number of years and didn't have to be told what to do. They were Gerry Callaghan from near Tralee in Kerry and Brendan McKenna from Listowel and were big strong men. Gerry was the bigger of the two and very, very strong. I worked with them for two campaigns and they were wonderful people to work with. They explained to me what the presses were for and how they worked. The lime pressers filtered the lime out of the juice. Lime from Staines was being burned in the factory having been brought in on the railway wagons and at some stage it was mixed with the juice and at another stage filtered out by the presses. The thick juice presses filtered out other stuff which was brown. When the press was full the lads would switch it off and open it. It consisted of about 40 frames pressed together with a sheet of very strong cloth on each frame. Each sheet would have to be lifted off with a handle for that job, dumped in a wheelbarrow and wheeled to the cloth washer.

Each cloth was very heavy because of the amount of strained silt on it and was sometimes very hot. Two thick juice presses and one lime press were changed in the day. My job was to put the cloths into the washer, then put in washing soda which was the same stuff we mixed with the bluestone when spraying. They were washed for a period of time, taken out and folded and left ready for the next press. Redressing the press had to be done very carefully and each frame pressed against the last one and when the last frame was done, the press was tightened up and was ready for use. I was kept busy, but it was easier than a long day in the bog or long days hay making. It was very warm there and all we wore were vests. The other two lads also wore clogs which may have been made in Charlestown at that time. When we went to the canteen at tea breaks we never wore jackets. On the coldest day of the year, it was a pleasure to get out into the cold and for the short while we were out we never got cold. It was a relief to know what one's job was and to know where one was going every morning and to know what one was doing. I knew nothing about the place before I left Ireland except for a few people who said the work was very hard and I wouldn't be able for it and I shouldn't go there. However, Padraic Durcan was in a different situation to me, we were spare men.

That year, they brought one hundred and twelve men over. Twelve of them were spare. The regular comers all went back to the job they had the year before. The jobs of the ones who didn't come were filled and then they had to find work for us. In my job, if Tom Bebbington was a younger man, it was possible they would have tried to manage with three men, but Tom worked all year in the factory. The work in the heat was a bit much for him, so I was fitted in there. In Padraic's case, he was put into a big store and told to tidy it up. The foreman was quite happy to have a man there, out of sight of the manager and he got what he wanted. A number of men would go there on the free pass and after one or two weeks' pay, would go off to a job in some other part of England.

Padraic, along with some others, was left alone. His father was a very intelligent man but had never been to England except perhaps picking potatoes, but he had worked for Mayo County Council for many years. It appears that he advised Padraic how to behave in the factory. His experience with the county council was that there would be five or six or more men doing a job for the council and they would be overseen by a ganger. Now the ganger was usually a nervous individual who was worried about losing his job and he would be watching his men like a hawk and if one of them stood up the ganger would get him moving again at once. Some of the men could play games with the ganger. One ganger was a very religious man and when the Angelus Bell went some of the men would down tools and start praying.

The trouble was, they didn't know when to stop. When the ganger would try to get them moving they would get carried away, pounding their chests and seeming very penitent. A funeral bell was another welcome relief. Another game they practiced when tea break was over was someone would come up with a scandalous story. That would grab the ganger's attention. Padraic's dad was very good at that. Tea break would go on for another quarter of an hour at least. However, the ganger was always on watch. After a couple of days, Padraic started getting very uneasy. Before he came to the factory his father had told him to watch the ganger all the time. He told me there was no ganger about and he must be sacked. He had great respect for his father and believed everything his father said. But his father didn`t know what he was talking about when it came to working in a factory. I tried to tell him he was OK and not to worry. Other older men there told him the same as I did. He was a very intelligent man but he took no notice. His father was the most important thing in his life, he had never been wrong and could not be wrong now. As time went on, he got more worried and stopped sleeping at night and didn't talk much to anyone. It was hard to watch the problem growing on Padraic. It was decided to send him home. When I came home in February, he seemed to be back to his usual self. If the father had gone to England with him, he would have been OK but the rest of his life was affected by that event. He died a young man in his forties.

When I got settled into the factory work, I was very happy. Everything was organised. We worked in shifts, 6 pm to 2 am in the morning (or this could be a 6 am to 2 pm shift). Then 2 pm to 10 pm in the afternoon and 10 pm to 6 am at night. The night shift was a bit difficult due to the fact that I was not used to sleeping in the daytime. After a couple of weeks of night shifts it was no problem and from time to time, one would have a very busy night so that would help to sleep better in the daytime. We got paid every week and sometimes the wage would be over £20 if one had overtime, and that was a huge change from life in Ireland. There was a nice group of people there. Most of them were regular older men who came there every year. There was a smaller number of young people like myself but they were also keen to advance their position in life. There were two or three people who had no interest in what they were doing, didn't want to work, and would try to make trouble if possible. They were found out over the first few weeks and were let go.

There were three pubs close to the factory. The Grove Hotel was at the railway station. The station had been closed before I went to England. The Plough was at a crossroads some distance from the factory and The Fox and Duck just down the road from the factory was another one we frequented. I remember a number of landlords coming and going in my time. They and their wives and families were very pleasant people but could handle any trouble that came their way. There would be some people from Ireland who had never been away before and who would act in a different fashion to English people but the publicans took it in their stride. The beer was different and cheaper than in Ireland. There wasn't much Guinness drank and they were not able to put a head on the pint like they did in Ireland but still some people continued to drink Guinness. I noticed a lot more women in the pubs also and of every age from the very young to great grandmothers. There was no television allowed. Card games and Dominos was played and of course darts. It seemed a very pleasant place where people could come for a couple of hours and have a few drinks, meet their friends, have a couple of games of whichever they liked and go home happy. Of course, there was the odd time someone would get drunk or a passing stranger would come in who had already consumed a lot of drink but there was never much trouble. Because of shift work, we couldn't spend much time in the pub which was a very good thing for us because when one couldn't have much drink one enjoyed it better.

The local shop was across the road from the Grove Hotel, and we would have to go there once a week at least because most of the men working in the factory would post money home almost every week. We had to use a registered letter where money was concerned and the lady who ran the shop was also the post mistress and she was very helpful in all sort of ways. She loved to converse and would ask a lot of questions about Ireland and she also knew everything about her local area. She was very much liked by everyone except her husband who ran away with some other woman. After doing our business in the shop, we would go across the road to the Grove where we would have a couple of drinks.

The landlord and his wife were friendly people and they had two dogs who were as close to being human as I have ever seen. The landlord worked in the factory also, not for the factory itself but for the Farmers Union. When a trailer of beet came into the factory, it had to be stopped at a building which was called the Toll House. There, a sample had to be taken from the trailer. We often got three hours overtime there, taking a bucket of beet from each trailer. The trailer door was opened. I held the bucket at the floor and another man would rake the beet into it with a drag. I would empty it into a system like a mini factory where it would be washed. There, a number of beets would be taken and have the waste blossoms chopped off and it went into something else which tested it for sugar content and other things. That is how the price was decided for the farmer and that is why the man from the Grove was there, to keep an eye on things for the farmer. When the landlord returned to the Grove after his day's work, the dogs would recognise the sound of his car and get very excited, rush out of the room, and return with two slippers and be waiting at the door to give them to him when he came in.

Another thing that was talked about a lot was the market in Wellington. It used to be held twice a week, on Thursdays and Saturdays. One day, myself, another lad whose name I don't remember now, and a lad from Galway called Ray Delargy decided to walk into town and see what it was like. It must have been after a night shift, otherwise we wouldn't have a full fine autumn day. We were advised to go to Wellington via Wrockwardine, a small English village which one would see in films and described in books. It was on top of a hill. It had a church with an old graveyard, a big house on its own, a scatter of smaller houses, a shop with an off licence but no pub. A bit further on there was a farm place where there was a very big manure pit and the liquid from it used to leak across the road. That reminded me of where many barns were at the roadside.

We got into Wellington and began to search for the market. My knowledge of a market was in the squares of Swinford or Charlestown. The pigs would be sold along the kerb in Bridge Street. They would be in donkey carts, sometimes with a cover over the crib.

There would be horse and donkey carts of hay and straw in the centre of the square and also bags of oats and sometimes barley. That was mostly sold for seed in the spring. Fowl and day-old chicks were also on the square and there would be a man selling delph. He would spread his stuff out on the square and was not worried that an animal would walk on it or a person. At that time, men would have an early breakfast before market, then they would have a few drinks and would get drunk quickly on an empty stomach.

It was not unusual to see men staggering and falling at a fair or market that time. The delph salesman would always be very witty and would keep a large crowd, mostly women, entertained. Sometimes, he would draw attention to some particular item and would put a price on it. Someone, perhaps a friend, would bid a much smaller price. The salesman would put on a show of being disgusted and very offended and would threaten to smash the beautiful piece of delph. Of course, he would get a much higher price and it may well have been bought by a woman who didn't need it all. On many days, there would be a very well-dressed man representing some church or other that was not the Catholic Church. He would be a very good speaker and would attract a large crowd. What he was saying was not much different from what was said at mass on Sunday, but he would be a much more able speaker. He could go on for a long time. The bus would come and take away some of his listeners, but others would join in. There was not much hope of him converting anyone but he was very entertaining. Those people never explained what religion they belonged to, but they were Christian. Anyway, the people of that time would not have a clue about any other religion.

However, going back to the market in Wellington, we could not find it. The town was crowded with people going every direction. We tried to follow groups of people a few times but they led nowhere. In the end, we asked someone where the market was and we found it, in a large walled off area away from the streets. There were stalls where clothes were sold. They were mostly run by Indians or Pakistanis. There was a large stall of second-hand clothes which a lot of the Irish workers were interested in because they would require working clothes, and others who had families at home would buy a lot of children's clothes and post them home in parcels. There were stores with heavy working tools like angle grinders and chainsaws and others sold radios and other stuff like that. There were builder`s shops doing a great trade and there were stalls selling all sorts of household goods. One that reminded me of home was the man who sold toiletries: soap, shampoos, ladies` face creams and beauty products. He used to auction stuff off. He was very witty like the delph man in Charlestown. He would have a large crowd around him and set one person off against another.

There were two book shops, selling second-hand books. I remember one in particular where an old woman sold books very cheaply. They were almost all very old hardback books of Shakespeare and Dickens and other famous writers. I wished that it was back home in Ireland and one could buy a library for almost nothing. We enjoyed our day there and I, for the first time, noticed the difference between the two countries. The crowds of people I ever saw in Charlestown or Swinford were only a fraction of what I saw in Wellington that day but unlike Charlestown where the people would be standing around and gossiping, in Wellington everyone was in a hurry.

I also noted the huge number of women with prams and children. In Ireland, women with babies would usually be mature, in their thirties and forties. In Wellington they, all of them, seemed to be in their teens. Most of them had a baby in a pram and one or more older ones running along with them.

We enjoyed our day at the market and left and after that, whenever we went to town, we always tried to arrange it for market day. I didn't know where Ray Delargy in the factory had gone and didn't hear anything about him until Christmas. A problem must have arisen because on Christmas Eve he was let go. According to a friend of his, Tom Flanagan, he walked out the gate singing "The Green Green Grass of Home". Tom Jones was at the top of the charts at the time.

I started reading about Shropshire a bit, but never got a book that covered the full history of the place. It was known as Salop and that address was still used in my time. Shrewsbury, which was the main town, was about nine miles from our factory. In the distant past the people were known as "the proud Salopians" and in the factory the locals always accused workers from Shrewsbury of being proud and having a posh accent. The accent of the local people was known as broad Salopian and when they would be giving out about somebody from Shrewsbury they would say, "I am going to tell Fred from Salop where to get off". The Romans occupied Salop for all the years they were in England and there are many remains of their work there. There are many famous places there. One is Ironbridge where the first iron bridge was constructed in the 1800s and a lot of Irish worked there building a power station, I think. The land was good and very well maintained, sort of rolling hills. There were no mountains that I could see, except for one near the factory. It was called The Wrekin, I never climbed it, and I regret that very much.

Almost everything in Shropshire had The Wrekin name involved in it. There was Wrekin Beer, Wrekin Haulage, Wrekin Machinery, Wrekin Healthcare. The name of the mountain was everywhere. There were famous people from Salop. Captain Webb, I think, got killed crossing Niagara Falls. There is a pub named after him in Wellington. There was also a writer, Mary Webb, whose books have been made into films. One of my foremen was Ken Webb, a very pleasant man. My charge hand said one day, "Ken's a tinker". I thought that meant he was a traveller, but the charge hand explained that the pipes in the factory carrying hot juice and water had to be covered to protect the workers from getting burned and also to keep the heat in. Ken would put wadding of some kind on the pipes and then encase it with a form of tin which he had to mould and join along the pipes. It was a very skilled job.

Another famous man was AE Housman. He was a poet and wrote a collection of verse called a 'Shropshire Lad'. He was from Staffordshire but when he came to Shropshire as a young lad he fell in love with the place. I had a small collection of his poems for many years but lost it somehow and would love to get hold of a copy again. There were lovely poems about the woodlands, the farming work, the seasons, the Romans and the Wrekin runs through it all. There was one poem called "The Lads That Will Never Be Old". It was about the young lads who worked on the farms and went to war and never returned. Shropshire was on the Welsh border and in the pubs at night, you would hear groups of people speaking the Welsh language. They seemed to be very fluent and it was very common during my time in England. I don't think there were any Welsh speaking areas in Wales like we have Gaeltacht areas in Ireland, but the Welsh seemed to love the language and they may have had a better way of teaching it than there was in this country.

Over here the method of teaching in school was abusive, more so where kids who were slower were concerned. We were not taught to love our language and at home parents hated it and seemed to be jealous of their kids knowing another language. That may go back to the time when their parents knew Irish and their kids didn't and were being talked about in a language they couldn't understand.

The four months passed quickly. The weather seemed to be always fine but of course when one is inside looking out, one would be thinking of all the work you could be doing if you were at home.

We got home in the beginning of February. We got by bus to Holyhead and boat to Dun Laoghaire. I thought that boat run was much rougher than the Liverpool route. It was very noticeable in the bar where men had trouble keeping their pints from spilling. Walking across the floor to a seat was very risky but they were very experienced drinkers and they never lost a drop. We got the train to Claremorris, and a bus to Swinford. There were a lot of people, wives and families, welcoming their men at the bus stop.

In my case, I went to Bolands and again got Mary Costello`s taxi home. My mother and aunt were in good shape and said the cattle were OK.

Jimmy Weever had dealt with the potatoes and fed the cattle. I had started sending milk to the creamery some years before that but the cows were dried off before I went to England. I got back into the old routine again. Cows started calving and I started sending milk to the creamery again. In March, Jimmy Weever and myself went to a few fairs and I think it was in Tubbercurry we bought a cow to increase my herd. She was a Friesian out of a Dairy Shorthorn. She was a heifer ready to calf and she did shortly after and I had no trouble with her. I think I paid £61 for her. I had her for many years after. She was the best cow I ever had. At peak, she would produce two gallons of milk in the morning and two gallons in the evening.

At that stage, I was sending up to three cans of milk per day to the creamery. The means I used for transporting the milk to the main road, where it would be collected, was donkey and cart. The donkey was the slowest donkey on earth and there was no way he could be speeded up. I was in Mick Dunleavy's in Charlestown one day. He ran a pub but he did blacksmithing and carpentry as well. I noticed he had an old pram there. It looked very strong and I asked him would it be capable of carrying a can of milk. He thought it would and he cut the front of the pram off to make it easier to push a can into it. I bought it and brought it home and tried it out. It worked very well for one can of milk, it was too small to carry any more. It was very smooth on the road and I would cycle almost as fast pulling the pram and one can as I could without it.

After a while the spokes in the wheels began to come undone but I replaced them with pieces of timber and it lasted all the years until I got a tractor. That year went very fast and it wasn't long until the time for going to England came around again. It was the same as the year before. We stayed in the Iveagh Hostel for one night and then continued to the boat and the factory. We went into the same jobs as the year before but it was well organised this time, and poor Padraic Durcan would not have had the trouble that upset him so much the year before. The four months went by quickly and I was home in February and back to the old grind. My mother told me there was a lot of trouble with the cattle over the winter. They were breaking out a lot. I knew I would not be able to go to England next year if that was to continue. What could I do about it? If I was here myself, I would be watching them all the time and would be able to identify weak spots. Some cattle are worse than others. I had a black cow who was very good at breaking out. One could fence off a stack of hay or a field where there were potatoes and oats and she would always get into it. She even opened the door of the barn once because she knew there was a bag of potatoes inside.

When reading The Farmers Journal one day, I came upon an article on fencing in New Zealand. I guess there would be very large farms there which would extend for miles. The New Zealanders had developed a new electric fence called the Waikato Electric Fence. It was effective for up to twelve miles. They used a strong steel wire and substantial fencing posts and very strong corner posts in particular. The wire was strained by a special type of strainer. When the fence was erected it was very strong on its own but when the electric shock was added to it, it was extra effective. The way the fence was constructed itself was strong enough to hold an animal back until it got an electric shock. The Journal said that Mullinahone Co-op in County Tipperary was selling the Waikato fence and all the other stuff required. It seemed to be just what I wanted so I contacted Mullinahone Co-op and they said they would supply everything I wanted. I forget what the cost was, but it was the best money I ever spent. All the gear arrived at the railway station in Swinford: the Waikato Electric Fence, four rolls of steel wire, a few boxes of insulators and staples and the wire strainer. I got Eddie Boland with the car, fitted the stuff into the boot and dropped it off at home. I got the stakes locally and had to dress them with Creosote to preserve them.

The next job was to get the fence erected. It was late harvest time and I would be going to England again at the end of September. I met Tom Burns one day and we talked about the job and had a look at the material involved, and as he had nothing on at the time, he said he would do the job. We planned out the whole thing and at the end, Tom knew how to do the job much better than I did. We started the job before I left for England and he finished it shortly afterwards. There was no trouble with the cattle that year, or any year after that.

Tom was an experienced electrician and, apart from that, he could judge a job better than most people. I was very lucky to get him at the time because he was thinking of what he should do in the future. The following year, he decided to go to England. He was a single man. He didn't own land so there was nothing to hold him here. He was a great friend of my father`s. They cooperated on many things, and he was my friend since childhood. Tom returned from England once for his father's funeral and I never saw him again after that. I understand he got married and had a family and I was informed of his death, at too young an age. That's life.

The next year in England was changed in a number of ways. For a start, there were three or four new people from the locality over with us. Frank Peyton from my village, who was also my old school mate, decided to give it a go. He had been to London working when he was sixteen, had come home for a while and then returned to London again. He was travelling to work early one foggy morning when he was hit on the head by another wagon and was very lucky to have survived. He was seven weeks in a coma, but then began to recover very slowly. After his time in hospital, he returned to his family where he recovered some more and began to ease his way back to work on the farm again. He never made a full recovery, but as far as conversation and wit was concerned, he was his normal self.

There was a young lad from Derrinacartha called Pat Tansey and another young fellow from Brosna called John Towey. We seemed to band together. I guess the fact that we knew people in each of our areas meant we could converse about them and also the fact that Frank could be very funny and witty added to the camaraderie. He could imitate Elvis Presley or anyone else if he decided to do them. When we settled in, I discovered that my job has changed. I had been moved from what was called the beet end of the factory to the sugar end. That was the end where it became sugar after it had been turned into juice in the centre of the factory.

There was an area called the 'Pan Floor' where there were five or six very high tanks called 'Pens'. The juice pressed from one to the other of the pens until it became sugar. It passed onto the next stage which was the 'Spinners'. The spinners were kind of tanks with no top or bottom. Those things spun at a very fast speed. The sugar, when it dropped into them, was very wet and brown and it fastened onto the walls of these tanks. A hose in the tank seemed to wash the brown, which may have been molasses, and the sugar became white. There was a man in charge of those tanks as they continued to spin and he would use a special fitting called a 'Plough'. He would put the plough against the inside of the tank and would plough the sugar off the inside of the tank and it would be moved slowly down to the bottom of the tank until it was empty. The sugar would fall onto a shaker and then onto a belt which would take it on to the sugar end.

Following that, there was a huge spinner machine called a 'Granulator'. The sugar dropped into this granulator and only the fine stuff got through. All the lumps were sieved out of it and would go down a pipe to be remelted. My job was to look after the granulator. If stuff backed up, I would clear it down the remelt. I also had to take a sample of sugar every hour and take it to the lab to be tested for whatever. Also, a lot of white sugar had to be remelted. It seems that sometimes the juice in the pans would go wrong and they would correct it by putting in a lot of white remelt sugar quickly. Another job I had to do on the ground floor, was to look after a pit where brown sugar was remelted. This sugar came from other factories where they didn't make white sugar. It came by train. The engine would push the wagon over the pit, a slide opened and the sugar would drop into the pit and a screw would take it into the system. There would be stoppages at times which I would have to clear and there would be overspills which I would have to shovel into the pit at the end of a load.

There was a very interesting group of people working on the sugar end. The man in charge on my shift was Jack Davies. He had worked in the factory all his life and he retired during my time there. He was highly respected by everybody working there and he also treated everyone with respect. The man I spent most time with, Cliff Croydon, came working to the factory every year at the same time as we did. He worked with carnival people all through the summer and operated two stalls. He was married and had two children. A lot of his friends in the carnival business, both male and female, also worked in the factory for the winter months. In fact, one of the women, Anne, married one of our men from Abbeyfeale in Limerick, Tom Flanagan. Most of the carnival people lived in a place called Oakengates on the far side of Wellington. They were great fun and it was a joy to work with them. My colleague Cliff was a wonderful guy. He could sing every Irish song I had ever heard of. He could tell stories all day. He had been in the army during the war and he could tell stories of that time also. There was never a dull moment.

On the night shift, there were four Irish lads stacking the sugar. The sugar was only bagged at night, therefore stacking had to be done at night. Con Piggot from Knocknagoshel in Kerry was the leading stacker, a second man was John Carey from Kerry also. I forget the third man as they would change on different years. However, I couldn't forget the fourth man. He was John Costello from Galway. He was another great character. It was said that the first year he came to England, he could only speak Irish. However, the year I got there he was very fluent in English and we had great conversations. A very long high crane was used in the sugar store and when the bags were taken off the belt and stacked on a type of pallet the chains of the crane were attached to the four corners of the pallet. The crane which was electric was situated up at the roof of the building and ran on rails from one end to the other. John Folan, Sean O'Culain in Irish, from

Lettercallow, Lettermore, Galway, operated the crane. He was also a great friend of mine. He ran a small farm in Galway. Where I would have a problem with wetland and drainage, he would have a problem with rock. When he was building his house, he had to have rock blasted to put in the foundation because the house would crack if the rock wasn't removed.

Also, when clearing fields or roadways, rocks had to be blasted. There was one other man who used to be involved with us, Nickie Tairis. He used to run the silos. The silos were two huge buildings about fifteen storeys high. Sugar went directly into the silos. As far as I know, when it was being bagged it returned from the silos and tankers of sugar were all loaded from the silos. They were just big fifteen storey tanks, but at the bottom of the silos there were rooms where everything was controlled. There were a lot of 'socks' hanging from the roof. These socks were tied up but when a sock was loosened, the sugar would begin to flow down from the silo. There would be a conveyer belt underneath the sock which would take the sugar to be bagged or loaded into a tanker or wherever it was supposed to go. Nickie Tairis was from Ukraine. He was captured as a prisoner of war by the British. He was taken to England and sent to work on farms but had to return to camp every night. Some English joker had told him that England was crawling with snakes especially in woods. As Nick used to have to cycle through a wood every night, he was terrified of being bitten and used to have nightmares of being bitten.

Over the years, he was released and then married an English woman. His fear of snakes faded from his mind but his new nightmare was that his wife would leave him. One night in the silo a string on a sock came loose and of course the sugar began to flow down. Nick had been doing some other job and didn't notice until perhaps a couple of tons of sugar had dropped down. He was afraid he would be sacked. There was no danger of that as he was a good and careful worker and the loss of sugar was a minor thing as it would be remelted again but Nick's nightmare changed from the fear of the wife leaving him to the fear of a sock becoming untied and filling up the room. My friend Cliff told Nick that when the room filled as high as the sock it would stop flowing but Nick didn't see the funny side.

There were quite a number of Ukrainians working in the factory. There was also a German, an ex-prisoner, there but he was a foreman whom we didn't have much to do with. When Jack Davies retired he was replaced by another Ukrainian, Nick Topiea. He was also a very pleasant man who told us many stories of his time in Ukraine during the war years. When the Germans invaded first, they ran before them and then when the Russian started winning they had to run before them. However, I think, and according to history I have read since, the Ukrainians disliked the Russians much more than they did the Germans and the young men who were not Jews were conscripted into the German army. Otherwise, they would not have ended up as prisoners of war in England. Nick Topiea was a married man in

Ukraine and when he was released and had a job he wanted to bring his wife back to England. The Russians would not agree to that, but it seems that in the end they came to some agreement and the next year I was over, she had come to England and had started working in the factory. I think Nick had owned a house. Otherwise, he would not have got her to England. According to his work mates, Nick had led a very quiet, comfortable life over the years but his wife carried out big improvements on the house and then sold it and bought another house. She was in the process of doing up the new house and planning to sell it again. Nick's life was much busier than it used to be. I found the sugar end of the factory was a very pleasant place to work with a mix of different people from all over the world.

Chapter 14

FARM DEVELOPMENT

When I returned home that year, everything had gone well. Seamus Groarke had looked after things for my mother that year. He was young, not long out of school. He was a great worker and he would be in England the following year and for the rest of his life after that. As the year wore on into late spring, I heard that my neighbours Mick and his wife Maggie Burke were going to sell their farm. It contained thirty-nine acres and would have been the biggest farm in the village for the first half of the century. At this point in time, Harry Peyton had bought two or three smaller farms and his son Tom would be farming about fifty or sixty acres now. Burkes` place would consist of about nine acres of very good land, four acres of not so good land and the rest was bog and part of that bog was owned by four neighbours who had the right to cut and save turf on it. I figured Tom Peyton would be in a position to buy it if he wanted it as he would have the money or at least the means of getting it. When it was put up for sale, no one was sure how much they wanted or how much it would go. Jack Stenson's place had been sold the year before. It consisted of two farms and two houses, one not lived in. It was bought by a young fellow from Killasser who was in the US and must have put quite a bit of money together. It was supposed to have gone for over four thousand pounds which was an awful lot of money in my eyes. However, some days after it went for sale, Tom Peyton called to me and asked me was I interested in buying the place. I said I would love to get the house and a few acres but I wouldn't have a hope of getting that much money together. He said we could split it between us, me taking the house, which was much better than my house, and five acres. He would have the rest. He suggested going to the bank and finding out where we stood. We agreed to do that so we had a meeting with the bank manager, who at that time was Dan O'Connell, a Kerry man. I don't know if he was a relative of the old Dan but he was a member of Charlestown Dramatic Society and I had seen him perform in plays. He was a very good actor and a very witty man also.

We explained our case and he said there would be no problem for me to get two or three thousand pounds. I had £1000 saved in prize bonds and the fact that I went to the factory for four months in the winter and had an increasing number of cattle meant that I should be OK. Things could always go wrong but one would have to take a chance.

The auction was on a particular day at a time which I forget now, a number of local people turned up but there did not seem to be any strangers or people who would be likely to be buyers. Johnny O'Hara from Swinford was the auctioneer. He was better known around the area as the pig buyer and he also sold furniture and carpets. He said a few words at the beginning, stating the price the Burkes wanted and asked would someone put a bid on the place, but no one did. We all stood around thinking for a little while. Then Tom and myself approached Johnny O'Hara and asked him could a deal be done. He spoke to the Burkes and the wife, Maggie (nee Durcan) said she wanted four and a half thousand, the same price as Stensons got for their place the year before.

Perhaps if it was left for six months or a year it would be sold for less but Tom and myself knew that Maggie was the boss and if it was left for any length of time, she would come to the conclusion that we were trying to wrong her and she would sell to someone who gave less money but that would be OK as long as we didn't get it. Maggie was not a bad sort of person at heart but her imagination could run wild and she had been known to fall out with neighbours over something she blamed them for which had nothing to do with them at all. Mick Burke, or Micheal de Burca as he was known in Tourmakeady where he came from, was a very nice man. He had worked in England and was in the Irish army for six years and had been a member of the guard of honour for ST O'Kelly when he was inaugurated as president. However, Maggie was the boss, the person we had to deal with, and we thought we were better off giving what she asked for so we agreed to the deal.

£2500 for each of us was needed. It doesn't seem to be much money now but in 1972 it was almost unthinkable for someone like myself who had no income except the dole and the old peoples' pensions. We got everything signed up with the lawyer (Kelly) and the Burkes sold off their stuff. I bought whatever things were in the house and I also bought one of the cows. That cow stayed at home on her own land but when her last cow was being sold Maggie got very emotional because I suppose she could see it was the end of her old way of life. She was fifty-three years of age at the time and had lived all her life on the land, apart from a few years in England. Her mother had died some years before and her father had died in 1945. She had two sisters. One was called Nell. I never knew her, but she was said to be a very friendly outgoing girl, who had gone to England and worked in a factory.

However, Nell got sick and came home and went into hospital here and after a period in hospital, died. She was supposed to have had TB. Maggie also was in hospital with TB, but she survived. The other sister, Sis or Julia, lived at home with the Burkes. There was talk of her getting married a number of times, but it never happened. Some years before the Burkes sold out, she ended up in hospital. The Burkes moved out during the summer and I got the key. I moved my mother and aunt into the house before I went to England that year. Owing debt, the amount that I owed was worrying. I could see all the things that could go wrong, like not been called to the factory. The cattle could go wrong, one of us could get sick and other things. That first year after I got the loan, I worried a lot. However, after I had paid my first couple of payments to the bank my mind was easier.

I finished that year in the factory, reclaimed seven acres of bogland and also levelled some fences to join fields together. My herd was getting bigger and I needed extra land. I was wondering what was the best way of reclaiming the bogland. Most of the bog had been cut off it over the past hundred years and there were signs that a past generation had tried to reclaim a small corner of it because one could see the tracks of ridges where potatoes had been sown. The way I saw land being reclaimed before, and only small areas were done, was by using a rotovator. This would dig up the land first and later one could plough and harrow and seed it. However, the seven acres I was doing was different because it varied from very level ground in one part, to soft, very wet ground, to very unlevel ground where there were banks of turf that a tractor could not drive over. I had been reading in The Farmer's Journal about a reclamation job that had been done in Kerry some months before. It involved the same kind of land as mine - a blanket bog, cutaway bog with red gravel-like subsoil underneath which would soak any amount of water. In Kerry, they used a large machine with a bucket on a long, outreaching arm. They used the machine to dig the ground with the bucket, leaving large buckets of earth containing an equal amount of bog and subsoil. After that it would be levelled allowing any surface water to soak down to the subsoil below. I began to enquire if anyone had these kinds of machines or did that sort of work. After a time I heard of two brothers, Michael and John McGuinness, from Lavagh, Ballymote, County Sligo.

Up until then, they would have been doing drainage work on rivers like the Moy which was being drained at that time. I must have phoned them because Joe McGuinness called to me and we walked over the land in question and he said they would do it. My trouble then was the fact that I had applied for a grant for only three acres but now that I had the opportunity to do seven acres, I needed a grant for seven acres. I contacted the government department in Claremorris. John Scally, the head of the department in Mayo, called to see me. We walked the land again and he was interested in the project but he talked of the problem of money being available within a particular year. He was a very pleasant man and enjoyed a joke and was very witty. I met him a few times after that but he died long before retirement. In the end he agreed to give me the grant for the seven acres. I forget now what the grant was, but it was a great help.

Sometime after that, the machine arrived on the low-loader driven by Milo Maye from Aclare. It was a very long truck and it was hard to find a turning point. The driver of the machine also came and he was Martin Mulroy from Meelick. They got it off the low-loader and into the field. It seemed a very big thing at the time to most of us who hadn't seen anything bigger than a tractor on the land. Martin called it a Hi-Mac and that particular type has survived down through the years and is in common use to this day. Martin started work and was here for a fortnight. We got to know each other well and had many interesting conversations and we still meet in Swinford from time to time. The job went well and there was only one small part of the field where the bog was too deep and the subsoil was too far down to mix but it was never a problem after. The next job was a great problem.

The field had to be levelled to make it suitable for seeding and the other work that followed. I was not keen to use a bulldozer because I was afraid it would compact the ground too much. I tried a few people with rotovators, but they thought it was too rough for them. Nothing happened until the factory work came round again in September, so I had to go without the job being done. However, while I was in England, my mother wrote to me and said a man called to her and said he was interested in the job. His name was James Horkan. I knew James well in the FCA. He was a Meelick man also. He was a young man and I didn't know he had started the agricultural contracting business. When I came home I contacted him. We had a look at the job and he said he could handle it. It would be very hard work because the tractor would be reversing almost all the time. He started the work and kept at it every fine day. It appears to me now that it didn't rain much in those years, or perhaps I don't remember the wet days. He finished the job in a short time and he worked very, very hard. Whatever money he got for the work was very well earned. The field looked lovely when it was finished. What was rough heathery bog last year looked like a large ploughed field now. The next work was the usual work of harrowing and seeding which Paddy Molloy did. Wills Brothers put out the lime, at two tonnes per acre, and also the fertiliser. I planted oats and grass seed and after a few days the sky was dark with crows and rooks and wood pigeons. They were picking up the oats seed and even if most of it was covered when the grain started sprouting, they would pull up the sprouts and find the grain on the end of them. I had a rifle at the time, but one would have to be very accurate to hit something moving. I borrowed a shotgun off Tom Peyton and hid behind a fence. I got a few rooks and pigeons but they were not afraid of being shot, so I had to forget about it and at that stage in my life, I was not fond of killing anything.

The oats grew well in some areas and not very well in other areas. The nature of the soil was poor and trace elements were missing. The good land had farmyard manure over the years and would have all the minerals required but this newly reclaimed land had never been used to produce anything but heather and wild grasses and mosses. When harvesting the oats, Tom Peyton suggested I get a binder from Fred Hughes who was an agricultural contractor living in Glantavrane, Kilkelly. Tom and myself went up for it one day and we discovered it was stored in one of the sheds of Tavrane House.

I remembered Harry Peyton telling me that he and his father James had gone to that house looking for a grant from Sir Henry Doran who lived there at the end of the 19th century and was in charge of The Congested Districts Board. When we were there, a farmer lived in the place. Some of it had been knocked down because there would have been high rates on the place. I heard later some wealthy person had bought the place and did it up. A few years ago I met a man in Swinford with Paddy Moran of Kilmovee and Gerry Murray and we got into conversation. I could tell by his accent he had spent many years abroad. He told me he now owned Tavrane House. He also told me that his great grandparents rented a small plot of boggy land in this area during or after the famine and they were evicted by Strickland or one of his agents. It was good to hear that story.

Anyway, we got the binder and got it working and cut all the oats. I later stacked it and it was fed to the cows by Tom Durcan who looked after the place that winter. The following year, I spread copper on the field but I noted that when the grass seed grew, it had a reddish colour and didn't look very lush.

I checked with what is now known as Teagasc and Michael Laffey, who was working in Swinford at the time, tested the field. I was advised at the beginning not to put too much lime on, as it was classed as bogland but the fact that it had been deep bog meant that there was probably more soil than bog in the mix. When I put out the lime, I had been advised to spread no more than two tonnes per acre. When Michael Laffey got the results of the test back, it needed eight tonnes per acre. He suggested putting four per acre the first year, and four again the following year. I did this. Sean Griffin from Carracastle did it both years and I saw the difference in the colour of the grass and also in better growth. I was told that the cause of the red colour and stunted growth was a lack of iron. When enough lime went on it released the iron. These seven acres added quite a bit to my arable acreage, but it took a number of years for it to reach its full potential.

Chapter 15

Last Days in Allscott

1973-74 would be my last year in England. My mother's sight had begun to get weaker. She got new glasses, but they were not much help. Tom Durcan, who had looked after the cattle for the past number of years, had some health problems, so I got Michael Harrington from Culmore to look after them in my absence. That year in the factory was a very good one. My foreman Basil Thatcher asked me to go on the stitching machine. It paid a higher wage than normal and it used to always be local English people who would do it. Cliff Croydon was doing the bagging. He could have got the stitching job but he didn't like it. We got on very well together and even though I enjoyed every year I was in the factory, I enjoyed this one the best. A lot of interesting things happened that year but I can't remember them now. I recall the work went on a fortnight longer than the other years. My mother was worried about that, but I felt I had to stick it out. I was very, very sad leaving because I had a feeling it would be my last. All the workers and all the management and a lot of local people I had got to know were wonderful and I could never say a bad word about them.

On the Irish side I missed John Folan and Con Piggot and others whose names will not come to mind at the moment. My local friends,

Frank Peyton, John Towey and Pat Tansey had not come over that year, but I still see them, except for Frank who has died.

On the English side there was Cliff Croydon who was better fun than all the comics on TV and films put together and Big Reg and the two Ukrainians and the foreman Basil Thatcher who was retiring that year and the sugar foreman, George Williams who had been a rear gunner in the RAF during the war and at times could lose his voice and could be very funny also. I had worked with a couple of black men from the Caribbean and the women in the canteen who were always very helpful. I enjoyed the publicans and the local people with whom one could have great conversations and learn about the way of life in England in the process.

Chapter 16

HOME CHANGES

When I get home, my mother's sight had failed more. She had been to the eye specialist, Doctor Laffey. He prescribed drops to be used several times during the day. Sometime in May, I think we went to the Eye and Ear Hospital in Dublin. I remember it well because that was the day the bombs went off in Dublin and a number of people were killed. I don't think she knew anything about that. However, they didn't, or couldn't, do anything for her in the Eye and Ear Hospital. She had the eye disease called Glaucoma. Nothing could be done except to apply the drops regularly. She still had some sight. She could go to town and walk around the land and work a bit in the house but she couldn't read which she used to like doing. Margaret Harrington, wife of Michael who looked after the cattle for the last year, used to help her in many ways and did so for the next four or five years. I continued with the farming. By this time, I had twelve or thirteen cows and the job was getting harder.

As the years moved on, my mother's sight got worse and she had to stop going to town on pension day. That was a great shock to her because she would meet her old friends and her own age group on that day. At that time, unlike now, there was plenty of public transport. A bus went to Swinford at 9 am in the morning. A bus came from Swinford to Charlestown at 1 pm. A bus went from Charlestown to Swinford at 3 pm and a bus went from Charlestown to Swinford at 6 pm. They were all Dublin to Ballina CIE buses and Charlestown was served very well with transport. People would come from outlying villages like Killeen, Killaturley, Barnacogue and even from Ballydrum and Tumgesh to catch the bus. There was one stopping point on the road called the Halfway Bush and a large crowd used to gather there at certain times like fairs and markets, Christmas and holiday times. Up to three buses would be laid on if a big crowd was expected. At times, the bus would be crowded with young men and women going to or coming from England and they would be in a happy mood whichever way they were going.

My mother always used that bus since that service started. She went in on the 1 pm bus and got out on the 3 pm. If she got delayed, she could come out on the 6 pm bus. There used to be a conductor on the bus at that time who knew where everyone got off and he was liked by all. My mother used a number of shops for her shopping every week. I guess that went back to the time of the ration books in the war years when one had to shop in a particular house. She always bought most of her foodstuff in Gallaghers in Church Street. They were known as Jimmy and Baby Tumour. I don't know what Tumour meant but I did hear the old people say that they had a sister who died of some wasting disease and that may be where Tumour came from. At some time in the past, the family came from our village and still have relations there. Next my mother would go to McCarthy's on The Square. At one time, that part of The Square was known as Bridge Street. McCarthy had been an RIC policeman and had married a sister of Baby Tumour. They had two sons, John and Jimmy. John became a barrister and fought an election in the 40s. In his later years he became a Judge. Jimmy remained in Charlestown and was supposed to take over running the parents` shop. It was a pub but they also sold bacon and some other things.

It was a busy pub with a snug looking out on to The Square. There was a strange sort of curtain on the window which seemed to be made of a light sort of material which would allow the people in the snug to see out onto The Square but the people out on the street could not see who was in the snug. Both men and women drank in there. Most people who travelled on the bus would have a drink there when they had their shopping done. They enjoyed being able to look on to The Square when there was a fair or market on and when there was an election on and there would be speakers shouting at people and at each other and still be seated and be able to enjoy their drinks. Then there was Webbs` Stall on the same street where the Webb Brothers Butchers sold meat. The stall had wheels on it but it was never moved in my time. The Webbs also had a shop in Bellaghy but did most of their business on The Square. Seamus Byrne had another butcher`s shop in Jack Peyton's house in Barrack Street but my mother mostly dealt with Webbs. Then there was The Post Office, also on Barrack

Street and run by the Harrisons, Val and his wife. They had one daughter, Anne, who was about my age. I noticed she had a tricycle. She was too young to handle a bicycle, but she could fly around on the three-wheeler. They also had a pub and pensioners would have a drink there. There were two clothes shops my mother used to go to. One belonged to Joe Mulligan on The Square who had two houses. He sold furniture from the other house. Joe was a very thin man. This was noted by the young lads going to the Eureka Cinema in which he was involved, along with his brother Luke. He was also an auctioneer and travel agent. The other clothes shop was Liam Kennedy`s on Barrack Street. He was a young man at the time and it is there she used to buy whatever I used to wear. There were two shoemakers or cobblers in the town. That was a very busy business in those times. One of the shoemakers was Joe White. He was in a house out on its own behind Bridge Street but my mother had never been to him.

My mother`s independence thus became much more limited by her poor vision and by being unable to go to town as easily. This development had also helped me to decide my days of seasonal work in England were now over.

Chapter 17

FULL TIME FARMING

I continued with the farming. By this time, I had twelve or thirteen cows and the job was getting harder. I decided to buy a milking machine. It was costly and took a large sum out of my annual milk cheque but it was the only way to go. My income would be much reduced by not having my four winter months in the factory. Every year since I had started farming, I had spent as much money as possible to improve and advance the farm. However, from now on, I would have to be much more careful. There was no other way of making money at that time other than off the land and I had come to realise that it would be very difficult to make a living wage off thirty-six acres of land. My neighbour Tom Peyton was making a living on the land but he had over one hundred acres and a herd of about thirty-five cows and other stock as well. In my case, I would need to have some other income if I was going to continue improving and reclaiming the place. I got the milking machine but first I had to set up a place in the old house. John Goldrick, who had returned from England to settle here, put in a floor in two rooms in the lower part of the house and did some other repairs. I was worried the cows would not take to it but when I got it installed they gave no trouble at all. I could milk two cows at a time and by putting four in while the first two were being milked, I could get the other two washed. It saved a lot of time and saved a lot of hard work. Sometime after that, I bought a tractor off Mick Gleeson. It was a 135 Massey Ferguson. It was a good tractor, easy to use and it lasted many years. I forget the price of it. I must have got a loan from the bank at the time but it was a very good investment because there were many things that could be done, in particular with the transport box and I would borrow some machinery from Tom Peyton from time to time.

I settled into life as a full-time farmer, following the rhythms of the year. Between the fields I had walked as a child and those I had bought and reclaimed, I knew every inch of my farm. I knew that I was doing the best I could with it. I took good care of my cattle and they provided me with a livelihood. I had good neighbours and friends. Although the work was hard and the hours long there was a contentment and an independence which might not have been available in a different way of life.

Martin Neary Snr with his mother Catherine Neary nee Durkan 1896

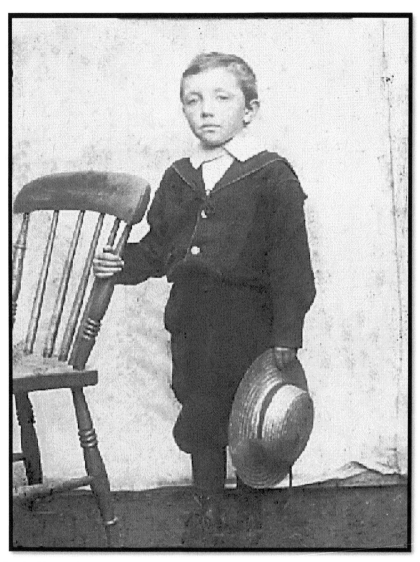

Martin Neary Snr 1898

Sitting Tom Gallagher (son of Breege Durkan and nephew of Catherine Durkan) Standing Martin Neary Snr (son of Catherine Durkan) and Tom Owen Gallagher's son of John Gallagher and 1st cousin to Martin Neary snr taken in Germantown, Philadelphia, USA 1916/17

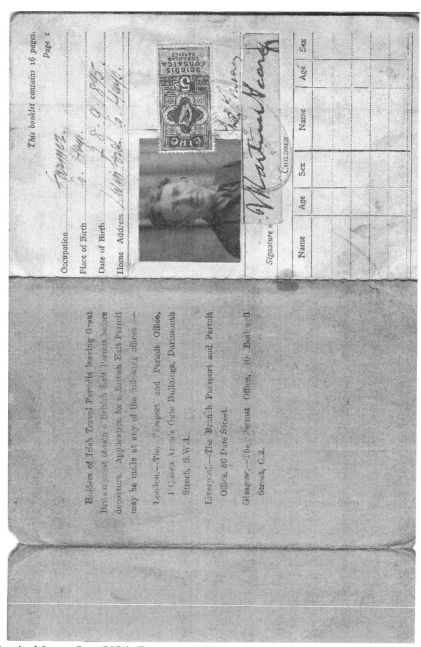

Martin Neary Snr. USA Passport 1914

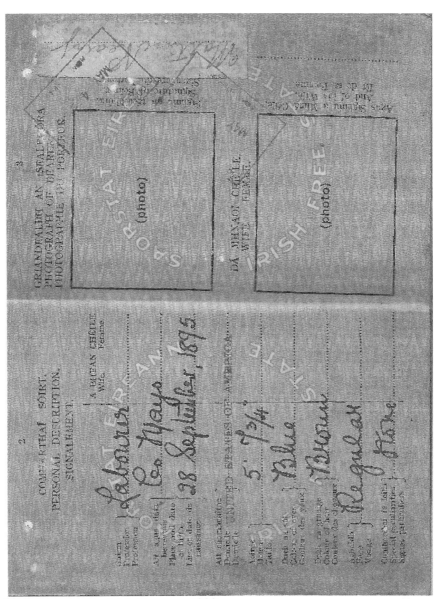

Martin Neary Snr. Irish Passport 1939

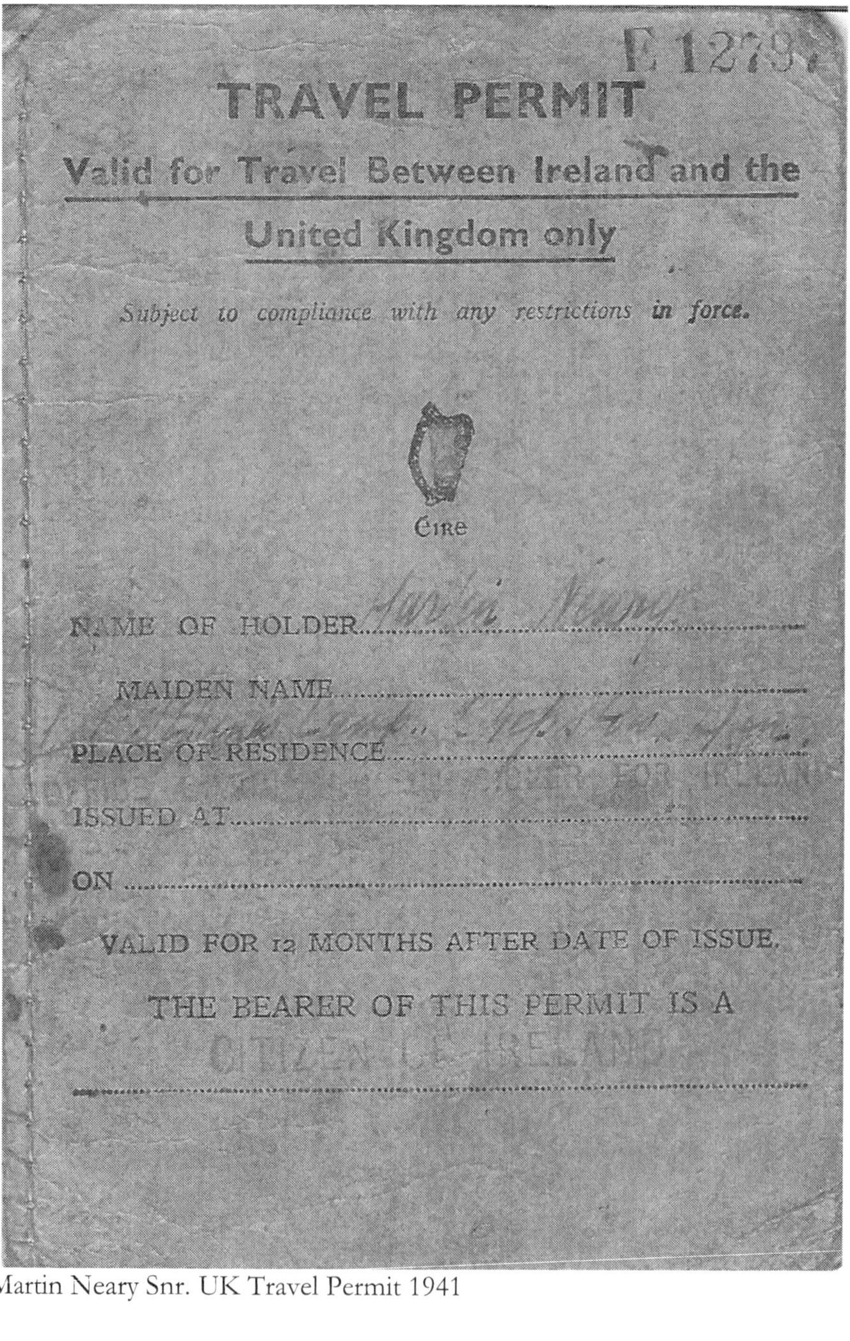
E 12797

TRAVEL PERMIT

Valid for Travel Between Ireland and the United Kingdom only

Subject to compliance with any restrictions in force.

Éire

NAME OF HOLDER Martin Neary

MAIDEN NAME ....

PLACE OF RESIDENCE ....

ISSUED AT ....

ON ....

VALID FOR 12 MONTHS AFTER DATE OF ISSUE.

THE BEARER OF THIS PERMIT IS A

CITIZEN OF IRELAND

Martin Neary Snr. UK Travel Permit 1941

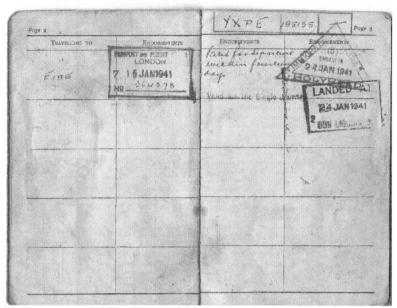

Martin Neary Snr. UK Passport and Travel Permit 1941

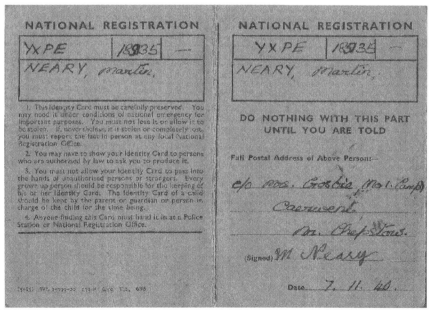

Martin Neary Snr. National Registration 1940